SCOTTISH
MILITARY
DISASTERS

PAUL COWAN

SCOTTISH MILITARY DISASTERS

Enjoy!

Paul

Neil Wilson Publishing Ltd
www.nwp.co.uk

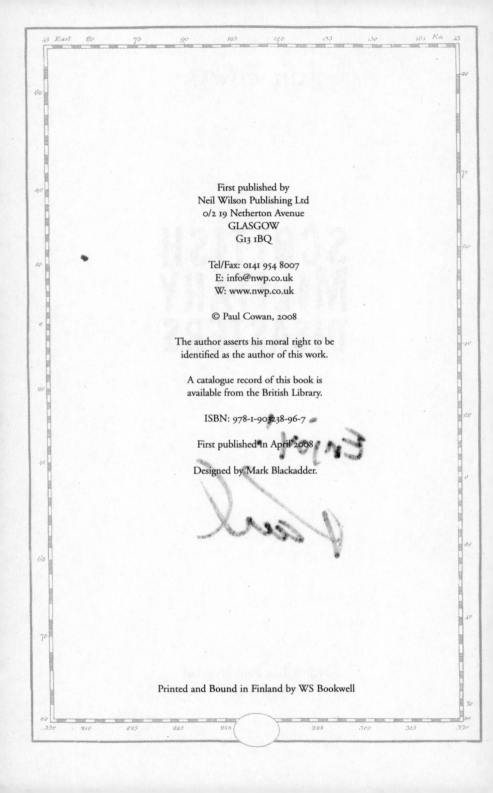

First published by
Neil Wilson Publishing Ltd
0/2 19 Netherton Avenue
GLASGOW
G13 1BQ

Tel/Fax: 0141 954 8007
E: info@nwp.co.uk
W: www.nwp.co.uk

A catalogue record of this book is
available from the British Library.

ISBN: 978-1-903238-96-7

First published in April 2008

Designed by Mark Blackadder.

Printed and Bound in Finland by WS Bookwell

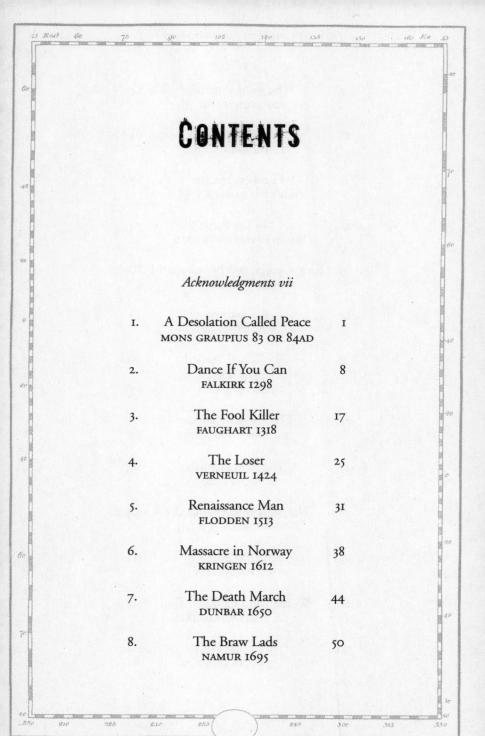

CONTENTS

CONTENTS

A Desolation Called Peace

MONS GRAUPIUS 83 OR 84 AD

The first Scot to be recorded in history was also the man who led his people to the country's first known military disaster. It is unlikely his countrymen knew the man the Romans dubbed Calgacus by that name. Nor would anyone have known their homelands would one day become a country known as Scotland.

The name Calgacus comes to us from the Roman historian Tacitus in his account of his father-in-law Gnaeus Julius Agricola's campaign against the northern British tribes in either 83 or 84AD. The exact year has never been determined because Tacitus's account is vague about when his father-in-law became governor of Roman Britain. Tacitus labelled the northern tribes as the Caledonii and even put a speech into the mouth of Calgacus condemning Roman imperialism before the climactic battle of Agricola's campaign. It is a speech that probably had more to do with Roman politics and the philosophy of Tacitus at the time than any actual words spoken by Calgacus.

> 'Whenever I consider the origin of this war and the necessities of our position, I have a sure confidence that this day, and this union of yours, will be the beginning of freedom for whole of Britain. To all of us slavery is unknown; there are no lands beyond us, and even the sea is not safe, menaced as we are by a Roman fleet. And

thus in war and battle, in which the brave find glory, even the coward will find safety. Former contests, in which with varying fortune, the Romans were resisted, still left in us a last hope of succour, as being the most renowned nation of Britain, living in the very heart of the country, and out of sight of the shores of the conquered, we could keep even our eyes unpolluted by the disease of slavery. To us who live on the uttermost confines of the earth and of freedom, this remote sanctuary of Britain's glory has up to this time been a defence. Now, however, the furthest limits of Britain are thrown open, and the unknown always passes for the marvellous. But there are no tribes beyond us, nothing indeed but waves and rocks, and the yet more terrible Romans, from whose oppression escape is vainly sought by obedience and submission. Robbers of the world, having by their universal plundering exhausted the land, they rifle the deep. If the enemy be rich, they are greedy; if he be poor, they lust for dominion; neither the east nor the west has been able to satisfy them. Alone among men they covet with equal eagerness poverty and riches. To robbery, slaughter, plunder, they give the lying name of empire; they make a desolation and call it peace.'

In his account, Tacitus also has his father-in-law make a speech to his men before the key battle at Mons Graupius. 'The most courageous of the Britons have fallen long since,' Agricola is reported to have said by Tacitus, 'those who remain are just so many spiritless cowards.'

Agricola arrived in Britain with the intention of conquering the whole island. The first Roman troops to arrive in Britain had landed with Julius Caesar in 55BC, but the Roman realised he would need more men than he had with him to conquer Britain and his visit was short-lived. The Romans arrived to stay in 43AD under the command of the Emperor Claudius.

Over the next three decades the Romans moved steadily north from their initial landing areas in south-east England. The conquest of Britain was for a time a priority for the Romans and at one point 50,000 troops, an eighth of the whole Imperial Army, were stationed there. Treaties with local tribal rulers were signed and puppet kings installed.

By the time Agricola arrived, in either 77 or 78AD, the Romans had control of Britain as far north as York. Agricola decided he wanted to be the man remembered in Roman history as the one who subdued the whole island and to accomplish this feat of arms he had four Roman legions at his disposal.

His first move was to crush a rebellion led by the Druids which had broken out in Wales around the time he first arrived in Britain. This was quickly done with an army of 20,000 men, which Agricola then marched north out of Wales to subdue north-west England. The north-east of England was next to fall and by around 80AD the Roman fleet and legions were probing as far north as Tayside.

The following year was spent tightening the Roman grip on southern Scotland by sealing it off from the unconquered north with a string of forts along the narrow 30-mile neck of land which separates the River Clyde in the west from the Firth of Forth in the east.

In around 82AD Agricola launched a lightning offensive across the country to finally conquer south-west Scotland. Then he began building another string of forts to seal the Lowlands from the Highlands. These forts controlled the mouths of the mountain glens linking the two parts of the country. The Roman fleet played a large part in Agricola's northern campaigns; it kept his troops supplied and allowed them to make surprise landings along the east coast of Scotland in support of the main army advancing north through Fife and Tayside.

The Caledonii could do little except retreat in the face of Agricola's disciplined and well-equipped legions and the more lightly armed Dutch, German and Belgian mercenaries who accompanied them. The campaign developed into a guerrilla war and

Agricola split his force into three columns in a bid to get to trap his elusive enemies.

But it was the Romans who were almost trapped. The Caledonii staged a daring night attack on the camp of the IX Legion in Fife around 83AD and managed to get inside its earth ramparts before their assault started to falter. Agricola was able to reach the base with reinforcements just before the Caledonii were about to overrun the Romans. The Caledonii broke off their attack as dawn was breaking and vanished into the hills.

That same summer saw Agricola's German mercenaries desert and steal three of his ships to take them home. The Germans sailed northwards and planned to plunder coastal communities along their route for supplies, but they found pickings slim and warriors from the coastal communities sometimes managed to drive them off empty-handed. Tacitus claims the Germans were forced to resort to cannibalism to survive. Eventually, after rounding northern Scotland, the German's poor seamanship saw the tiny fleet shipwrecked and the survivors enslaved by local tribesmen.

Meanwhile, Agricola was continuing his march northwards along the east coast of Scotland. However, his success was uniting the northern tribes as they had never been before and by the following year the Caledonii had collected an army Tacitus says numbered 30,000 men. Agricola's force may have numbered as many as 20,000 men.

The site of the battle where the two armies clashed has never been positively identified. Using Tacitus's description of the fight, some experts have placed the Battle of Mons Graupius as far south as Perthshire, while others believe it was fought just east of Inverness, near Huntly. Wherever it was, Agricola built a temporary fort there and next morning his troops awoke to find an army commanded by the man Tacitus calls Calgacus waiting outside it for them.

The leading troops of the Caledonii army were drawn up on a plain in front of the Roman camp. Behind them, a large force of warriors stood on the slopes of the mountain Tacitus dubbed Mons Graupius. Agricola decided to use his 8,000 mercenary troops for his first attack on the waiting Caledonii. The mercenaries carried short stabbing swords and javelins, while the Caledonii were armed with small shields and long blunt-tipped swords intended for slashing rather than stabbing.

The battle opened with an exchange of stones and javelins between the two armies; the Roman army's shields staved off the stones and the Caledonii were able to bat away the javelins with their three-and-a-half-foot-long swords. The mercenaries then charged the Caledonii and in the tightly packed close-quarter combat that followed they had the advantage with their short stabbing swords.

The Caledonii also had chariots but these clumsy vehicles were out-manoeuvred by the Roman cavalry and routed. The Roman horsemen then launched a charge to support the mercenaries but against mounted troops, the Caledonii's long swords were now an advantage and they were held at bay.

The Caledonii who were lined up on the slopes of the mountain then started to come down in a bid to get behind the Romans but Agricola had expected this and kept four squadrons of cavalry back to deal with just such an attempt. The cavalry swept down on the advancing warriors and quickly had them on the run. The horsemen then wheeled around to join the attack on the Caledonii still locked in battle with the Dutch and Belgian mercenary troops.

What little discipline and organization the Caledonii had had up to this point now collapsed and warriors began fighting their own personal battles; some launched suicidal attacks on the nearest group of Romans, others chose to run. The battle degenerated into slaughter with the Romans beginning to kill their Caledonii prisoners when their numbers grew too great to handle but some Romans proved too enthusiastic in their pursuit of the fleeing Caledonii and found themselves ambushed in nearby woodland.

The main Roman advance across the battlefield was by now systematic and before long the pockets of warriors trying to hold out amongst the trees were surrounded and killed. The battlefield itself was soaked in blood and covered in body parts. Around it, smoke could be seen rising from the farms and villages the fleeing Caledonii were busy torching, to deny supplies to the Romans. Cavalry patrols failed to find a single living soul for miles around the battlefield.

Tacitus claims 10,000 Caledonii warriors were killed that day for the loss of 360 Romans. Though the figures have to be taken with a large pinch of salt, it was a major defeat for the northern tribes. All of Scotland lay at Agricola's feet. However, winter was fast approaching and the final conquest would have to wait until the following year.

It never happened. The Emperor Domitian in Rome saw the victor of Mons Graupius as a potential rival for imperial power. Agricola was recalled to Rome and his career was stalled. He died in 93AD at the age of 56; Domitian is suspected of ordering the poisoning of the man who had come so close to the final conquest of Scotland. Agricola's work was soon undone. The forts he had built on the Forth-Clyde line were abandoned as troops were withdrawn from Britain to fight elsewhere.

In around 118AD, the IX Legion, which had almost come to grief at the hands of the Caledonii 30 years before, was sent from its base at York to deal with fresh unrest in the north and was badly mauled. Until recently, it was widely believed the IX Legion had been wiped out somewhere in Scotland, but recent research suggests it survived and was sent to garrison what is now Holland.

The losses inflicted on the IX Legion and the continued turmoil in northern Britain led to a momentous decision; the Emperor Hadrian ordered the construction of an 80-mile-long fortified wall from the Solway Firth in north-west England to the River Tyne in the east. It took from 122AD until 128AD to complete the wall which divided the subdued south from the unconquered north. But the Romans had not given up completely on northern conquest. In 142AD a 37-mile line of forts linked by an earth rampart was built between the firths of Forth and Clyde. However, this fortification, known as the Antonine Wall, was abandoned after about 20 years and the northern frontier of the Roman Empire once again became Hadrian's Wall. There were greater threats to Rome by that time than the warrior tribes brooding away in the forests and mountains of Scotland.

Perhaps, by losing the battle at Mons Graupius, the Caledonii actually won the war against Roman conquest. If Agricola hadn't won such a stunning victory, he may not have been recalled to Rome and would have completed his conquest of northern Britain the following year. History may have been drastically changed and Scotland, as we know it, might never have been. Sometimes to lose the battle, is to win the war.

DANCE IF YOU CAN

FALKIRK 1298

Who knows what would have happened if William Wallace had defeated the English at Falkirk in 1298? He probably would not have been disembowelled alive and then hacked into pieces for public display. Perhaps Robert the Bruce would never have risen to prominence and, as king of Scotland, finally driven the English out? But could Wallace have achieved independence for Scotland if he had won at Falkirk?

The Scotland that Wallace briefly led against the English occupation was a deeply divided country. Its political leaders were a mixture of the descendents of Celtic warlords and the Anglo-Norman nobles brought to Scotland by King David I after he was crowned in 1124. David was anxious to prop up his powerbase with the services of some of the finest armoured cavalry in Europe and to modernise his realm by imposing the highly structured feudal system on Scotland. The Anglo-Normans, many of whose families had arrived in England with William the Conqueror, in turn married into David's family and the Celtic nobility to consolidate their grip on the country.

The Anglo-Normans in Scotland were a real problem. Many had estates in England and France in addition to their lands in Scotland. Patriotism was a foreign concept to these men, whose driving interests were personal wealth and power. The chance for one of these lords to actually rule Scotland came following the death of King Alexander III in 1286. The king's lust for his new wife overcame his common sense when he ignored his courtiers' advice not to attempt the ride from Edinburgh during a violent storm to join her at her palace in Kinghorn in Fife – his body was found with a broken neck at the bottom of a sea cliff near Kinghorn.

Alexander's only heir was his four-year-old granddaughter Margaret in Norway; her mother, Queen Margaret of Norway, had died giving birth to her. She was sent for but the little girl died from illness shortly after arriving in the Orkney Islands. The Scottish nobles, who would have run the country until Margaret was old enough to assume the reins of power herself, had been working on a scheme which would have married her to the son of King Edward I of England. The English kings had long claimed that the kings of Scotland owed allegiance to them, but they had never backed up this assertion with a full-scale invasion. That changed when Edward I came to the throne in 1272. Edward soon proved to be an able king and a good general. He dreamt of ruling the whole of the British Isles and his first move was to conquer Wales.

The death of little Margaret made it look as though an invasion of Scotland might not be necessary. The Scots nobles asked Edward to decide who their next king should be, like a flock of sheep asking a wolf to become their shepherd.

There were 13 claimants to the Scottish throne and the two main ones were Anglo-Normans, Robert Bruce and John Balliol, who both claimed descent from David I, Alexander III's great grandfather. Both men had extensive estates in England and already paid homage to Edward, another Anglo-Norman, for these. They both agreed to acknowledge Edward as overlord of Scotland when he decided which man should be king. To Balliol and Bruce, Scotland was just another piece of real estate.

Edward appointed 104 assessors, 24 English and 80 Scots, to weigh up the legal merits of all the contenders' claims to the Scottish throne and make their recommendation to him for a final ruling; Edward came down in favour of John Balliol in November of 1292. It was a perfectly legitimate decision but the appointment suited Edward well because Balliol was a weak man. Soon Edward set about humiliating the new Scottish king and making it clear that he was regarded as a vassal of the English throne. Balliol was summoned to London to answer petty legal complaints from Scots who had gone over his head to Edward for judgements.

The final straw came for Balliol when Edward declared war on France and demanded the Scottish king and his nobles come south to serve in the English army. War with France was not in Scotland's economic interest because the country's main export was wool sent to Flanders; Edward's war would close that market so Balliol refused to answer Edward's summons. Balliol also prepared an army against England.

Edward was outraged at Balliol's defiance and marched north to seize Scotland's largest city, and main trading port, at Berwick-on-Tweed; the city was defended by a moat and wooden palisade. Perhaps the Scots were ill-advised when they lined the palisade to bare their buttocks at Edward and his troops, but that was no excuse for the orgy of murder and arson with followed Berwick's capture by the English. Thousands of Scots were killed and thousands more fled north as refugees from the carnage Edward had unleashed on the city. Edward ordered the rebuilding of the city and had it heavily fortified; English settlers were sent north to colonise the area.

Balliol's army was defeated a short time later near Dunbar and he was deposed and jailed by Edward. After several years of imprisonment, Balliol, known to the Scots as Toom Tabard ('Empty Coat') was released and died on his French estate in 1313.

With no one to stand in his way Edward now declared himself king of Scotland and demanded the Scots nobles put their allegiance in writing in a document which came to be known as the Ragman's Roll. One man who did not sign it, because he was not important enough, was William Wallace. He steps into history at the age of about 26 and little is known about him except that he came from minor gentry who held land in either Renfrewshire or Ayrshire.

Edward appointed a colonial administration which quickly

alienated the Scots through its brutality and the Scottish Anglo-Normans were angered to find all the plum jobs were going to their English cousins. The English were soon garrisoning all the key castles in Scotland and building a chain of smaller wooden forts around the country to tighten their grip on it.

It was not long before the Wallace family fell foul of their new English masters. William's father Malcolm is said to have been killed in a skirmish with the English and the English are also accused, in some accounts, of murdering Wallace's wife. English accounts from the time consistently describe Wallace as a thief and a bandit, but the line in those days between outlaw and freedom fighter was often very blurred (as it is today). One thing is certain: Wallace tapped into a feeling of Scottish nationalism which few of the country's nobles shared, or perhaps even understood.

The turning point for Wallace came when he killed the English Sheriff of Lanark, William Hazelrigg, in 1297. Wallace is reported to have hacked the Englishman into pieces; a description that may be due to English propaganda, or it could be true. Whatever, there was no turning back for Wallace after that and Scots flocked to join his fight to free their country from English rule.

Wallace first declared that he wanted to restore Balliol to the throne; a move that did not endear him to the Anglo-Norman nobility in Scotland. There were other resistance movements in Scotland but not all were pro-Balliol. The Bruce family made sure that they had men fighting on both the Scots' side and the English.

Wallace joined forces with an army of rebels from northern Scotland led by Andrew de Moray. Together, the pair formed a formidable threat to English rule and it wasn't long before Edward's Governor of Scotland, John de Warenne, and his chief tax collector, Hugh de Cressingham, were leading an army to crush the rebels.

The two armies met on 11 September 1297 near Stirling, a town that controlled one of the main gateways between northern and southern Scotland. However, the English badly underestimated the mainly peasant Scottish army. The Scots had taken up a strong position on the high Abbey Craig (the site of the current Wallace

Monument) overlooking the causeway crossing the flood plain down to the narrow wooden bridge which crossed over the River Forth to nearby Stirling Castle. Both De Warrene and de Cressingham ignored suggestions that part of the English army should cross the river upstream at the Ford of Drip to cover an English advance over the bridge.

De Warrene then decided to cross over the bridge into the loop of land that was hemmed in by the River Forth: an arrogant decision he would soon regret. The cavalry then began to feed through the narrow choke point formed by the bridge in the face of the enemy; the English commanders thus making it clear they held the Scots in contempt. Only two fully armoured knights could ride side-by-side at a time. Wallace and de Moray waited until half the cavalry had crossed.

Then, armed only with spears and axes, the Scots rushed down the hill to engulf them.* The rest of the English army could only watch helplessly from the other side of the river as the knights were butchered by the Scots. Unable to cross the bridge in any numbers, if at all, the English retreated, leaving their comrades on the far side to their fate.

The English army did not stop retreating until it was back south of the border. The English may have lost up to 100 men-at-arms and 5,000 infantry at Stirling Bridge; amongst them was de Cressingham, whose body English propagandists insisted was flayed and turned into leather straps and belts by the Scots.

Edward's hold on Scotland had been broken, though the English still held several key castles. But the Scots had suffered one very serious loss at Stirling; Wallace's fellow Guardian of the Realm, de Moray, who some argue was the real brains behind the victory, had been badly wounded and was dying. Wallace was confirmed as sole Guardian of the Realm; after all, he was very popular with the Scots peasantry and many of the Anglo-Normans preferred to keep a low profile rather than risk Edward's wrath by taking a leading

---

* Until this battle, mounted cavalry had never been defeated by spearmen anywhere in Europe.

part in the rebellion. Wallace also had the advantage that the various noble factions would rather see him as Guardian than one of their rivals.

Wallace, now declared Sir William, possibly by himself, took the war into England and laid waste several northern counties before retreating back into Scotland. Burning and pillaging on the enemy's side of the border was to remain a common feature of the wars between Scotland and England for several centuries to come. Edward knew he would have to deal with Wallace himself. He gathered 2,000 of his best and most reliable knights and 12,000 infantry and archers for an invasion that began in early July 1298. The shock of a charge by armoured knights was still the main battle winner in the Europe of the time and the Scots use of 12-foot spears to ward off the charge was a battlefield innovation ahead of its time. Sadly, Edward was also a brilliant tactician and had brought a large force of archers armed with longbows; the use of these in battle was an innovation that would serve the English well for two centuries.

Wallace wisely decided to avoid battle with the English if he could and the campaign turned into a game of cat-and-mouse as the Scots manoeuvred around southern Scotland one step ahead of the English. Miserable weather and poor supply lines, largely due to Wallace ensuring a scorched-earth policy, hampered Edward's movements and before long his Welsh troops were on the verge of mutiny. Edward released 50,000 gallons of wine to the Welsh in an ill-advised attempt to restore their morale. Instead the Celts went on a drunken rampage and killed several English priests. Order was only restored when the English knights charged into the Welsh and killed about 100 of them.

Edward was camped near Linlithgow and was considering retreating back to Edinburgh for fresh supplies when two treacherous senior Scots nobles, the Earls of March and Angus, appeared and told him that Wallace's army was only 15 miles away, near Falkirk. Edward quickly had his army on the march, but when he arrived at the Scots camp he found it abandoned. When Wallace learned the English were on their way he moved his troops to a stronger defensive position. Why he didn't continue his policy of avoiding battle is not known, but perhaps he felt that to keep the momentum of the rebellion going, he now needed a victory.

The Scots were formed up on a slope with Callendar Wood behind them and the boggy Westquarter Burn in front of them. Wallace had drawn them up into four giant spear-bristling hedgehog formations of between 1,500 and 2,000 men each. Wooden stakes had been hammered into the ground around the four rings of spearmen, known as schiltrons, to further hinder the expected charge of the English knights. Between the spearmen, Wallace placed his archers; a small force of Scottish knights on horseback was held in reserve. Wallace is reported to have told his troops, 'I have brought you to the ring, dance if you can.'

The English, as expected, opened the battle with a thundering charge by one of three divisions of knights. The solid mass of steel and horseflesh mired in the bog in front of the Scottish position but managed to make its way out again to charge at one of the schiltrons. The second division of knights avoided the bog and also charged one of the schiltrons. The Scottish archers, caught outside the schiltrons, were quickly massacred, but the knights could make little impression on the tightly packed rings of spears themselves.

The Scottish cavalry, made up mostly of minor nobles and their followers, fled almost before their English counterparts could reach them; treachery has been suggested, but it was just as likely to have been cowardice. The disappearance of the Scots cavalry meant that Edward could bring his archers up unmolested.

A skilled man with a longbow could loose 12 arrows a minute and soon a hail of steel-tipped death was raining down on the Scots spearmen. The Scots had to stand and take it and soon they were being cut down in their droves. Once the Scots ranks were sufficiently depleted, Edward unleashed his third division of knights and this time they had little problem smashing open the schiltrons. The Scots died in their thousands while only two English knights of any consequence had been killed. Records kept by Edward's financial bookkeepers show 100 English knights billed the king for horses killed by the Scots during the battle.

Wallace joined the rest of his army fleeing the slaughter and quickly resigned the Guardianship. He does not appear in history again until August 1305 when he was betrayed and handed over by the Scottish Earl of Monteith to Edward. Wallace may have been abroad in the intervening years or he may have gone back to fighting a small-scale guerrilla war against the English.

What is in no doubt is what happened to him once he was in Edward's hands. Edward staged a mock trial at Westminster in which Wallace was accused of treason and various war atrocities, including murdering nuns. The guilty verdict from Edward was a foregone conclusion and he was sentenced to the traditional barbaric execution English royalty reserved for people who really irritated them.

Wallace was crowned with a laurel wreath and dragged through the streets of London by horses to Smithfield. There he was strung up on a gallows until he was semi-conscious and then slashed open for the removal of his entrails, which were burned before his eyes. Decapitation must have been a welcome end to the agony that had been inflicted on him. Wallace's head was put on display on London Bridge and his arms and legs were each sent to Newcastle, Aberdeen, Berwick and Perth for exhibition.

However, Edward's victory at Falkirk and torture of Wallace had failed to force the Scots into meek submission to his rule. The Anglo-Normans now tapped into the vein of peasant patriotism Wallace had revealed and the Scots nobles revolted again in various incestuous combinations. The Bruces had survived Edward's wrath so far by playing both sides in the revolt, but now they threw their lot firmly in with the rebellion. Robert the Bruce, grandson of the Bruce who stood against Balliol for the throne, murdered his main rival for the Scottish leadership, John Comyn of Badenoch in 1306 in Greyfriars Church in Dumfries, and declared himself king.

Scotland was plunged into a conflict which was both a civil war and a war of national liberation. Edward, now 68-years-old, was marching north to crush Bruce when he died at Burgh Sands near

Carlisle from exhaustion and dysentery in 1310. His tomb at Westminster Abbey proclaims him 'Hammer of the Scots'.

Edward's son, Edward II, was not half the politician or warrior his father had been. Bruce and his spearmen beat the new English king and his army at Bannockburn in 1314. By 1323 Edward II, with England wracked by civil strife, gave up his attempts to reconquer Scotland and asked for a truce. Scotland's independence was formally recognised by the Treaty of Northampton in 1328.

Would independence have come without Wallace? It's hard to say. He kept the flame of independence burning when the Anglo-Norman Scots nobles were willing to let it to go out. But peasant power alone was never going to be enough to win independence. Wallace, unlike Bruce, never claimed to be king although a king was what the Scots nobles wanted and needed. The whole structure of power in Scotland revolved around the nobles' relationship, or lack of it, with the Crown.

Wallace's populist rebellion had threatened that balance of power within Scotland as much as it had threatened English rule.

It is doubtful that Robert Bruce shed any tears for Wallace.

THE FOOL KILLER

FAUGHART 1318

The assassin masquerading as a village idiot did not hesitate as he brought the ball and chain down on the head of Edward Bruce, smashing his victim's skull to pieces. The self-proclaimed king of Ireland, and brother of Scotland's liberator from English rule, was dead. That, at least, is one of the versions of how Robert the Bruce's younger brother Edward died in 1318 but the truth is lost in the mists of time and the thick black clouds of medieval propaganda. Being killed by an assassin playing the fool somehow seems a fitting end for Edward Bruce.

Edward was the Scottish king's only surviving brother after ten years of war to end the English occupation of Scotland. Three other Bruce brothers, Neil, Alexander and Thomas, had been executed by the English. Edward Bruce was undoubtedly a brave man but he was also lacked the judgement of his elder brother. A misplaced sense of chivalry had led him to make a deal with Sir Philip Mowbray, the English commander, to end his siege of Stirling Castle, the last major Scottish fortress still in English hands. The basis of the pact was that Mowbray would surrender if any relieving English force failed to arrive within nine miles of it by Midsummer's Day 1314. Robert was not impressed with this arrangement, but accepted it.

After years of successful guerrilla warfare aimed at squeezing the English out of Scotland, the last thing Robert the Bruce wanted was pitched battle against the flower of English chivalry. The last major battle the Scots had fought against a large English army, at Falkirk in 1298, had resulted in a massive defeat. Robert had deliberately been avoiding a head-on confrontation, but Edward's offer now set the Scottish army of peasant spearmen on a collision course with the biggest and best-equipped English army ever to have invaded Scotland.

Luckily, the English victor at Falkirk, Edward I, was dead and his son Edward II was not half the warrior or general his father had been. The English army was routed by Bruce and his spearmen near Stirling at Bannockburn; the English forces surrendered and Stirling Castle was back in Scottish hands once more. Many commentators describe this as Scotland's greatest military victory. It might have been, but Scotland did not gain peace after it; the conflict continued.

Although Robert the Bruce found himself undisputed ruler of Scotland as a result of the battle, his brother Edward wanted his share of power. Scotland was not going to be big enough for the two Bruce brothers; the answer to the king's dilemma came from Ireland.

The English had invaded Ireland in 1171, after first being invited there as mercenaries by the warring tribal kings who between them controlled the island. Since then Ireland had been a cauldron of conflict for all concerned; the native Gaelic princes fought both each other and the English interlopers for control; the Anglo-Norman knights who had crossed the sea to Ireland in search of an easy land-grab were bitterly disappointed and, as well as fighting the Irish, began fighting each other; the English Crown back in London faced an uphill fight to control the Anglo-Norman knights and the Royal Writ did not count for much outside the trading city of Dublin; a further complication came from Anglo-Norman knights who married into the Gaelic petty 'aristocracy' to strengthen their own land claims.

The Bruces' success in kicking the English out of Scotland made some Irishmen wonder if they could do the same for them. There was a precedent for bringing in an outsider; in 1263 a group of Irish princes offered the high kingship of the island to King Haakon IV of Norway in the hope he would drive the English out for them. However, Haakon was too busy fighting the Scots for control of the Western Highlands and Islands to take up the offer, and his defeat by them at Largs in 1263 ended his chance of being high king of Ireland.

Robert the Bruce saw Scottish intervention in Ireland as a possible way of destabilizing England and furthering his struggle for undisputed Scottish independence. The English defeat at Bannockburn had not resulted in formal recognition of his kingship and there was still a chance Edward II would stage another invasion. The Anglo-Normans in Ireland had long been suppliers of soldiers and supplies for the English armies fighting in Scotland and an invasion would hopefully knock them out of the war. A successful takeover of Ireland could also prove a springboard for an invasion of England via Wales.

The obvious man for the intervention in Ireland was Edward Bruce. He had proved a reliable, if hot-headed, commander during the war against the English occupation and had a claim to royal blood through his descent from King David I of Scotland. Best of all, Robert would be rid of his interfering brother who was proving a liability at home. While Robert had a certain charm, a velvet glove hiding his mailed fist, young Edward was a boor. Sending Edward to Ireland would kill several birds with one stone.

Near the end of May 1315, Edward Bruce landed at Larne with a force composed of Scottish veterans of the long war against the English. Waiting to meet him was one of the most important of the native Gaelic kings in the north of Ireland, Donal O'Neill of Tyrone. The only other Irish leader of any consequence to greet Edward at Larne was Robert Bissett, Lord of the Glens of Antrim; the Bissetts were Scots by descent. Edward Bruce's arrival in Ireland took the English administration in Dublin by complete surprise. It could well be that the landing also caught the native Gaelic leadership unawares, as few appear to have supported O'Neill's offer of the high kingship to Edward.

The Scots, said to number 6,000 men, easily routed a scratch force raised by English landowners in north-east Ireland and chased it to the castle at Carrickfergus. Safe behind the stout walls of the castle, the English barons mocked the Scots and Edward vented his frustration by burning down the nearby church where most of the population of the town of Carrickfergus had taken refuge. Burning a church filled with frightened people hardly endeared Edward and his men to the local population and nor did it encourage the Irish to flock to the Scots' banner.

Edward left a small force to keep the English cooped up safely in Carrickfergus and set off south towards Dublin with the rest of his army. They defeated a force of pro-English – or should that be anti-Bruce – Irish troops at the Moiry Pass before burning the town of Dundalk to the ground. The Scots chased down every Englishman they could find in Dundalk and murdered them.

A famine in Ireland at the time meant that food was scarce and the Scots had little choice but to pillage what little food was available. Irish chroniclers claim that famished Scots dug up the dead and feasted on their bones. The Scots soon faced their greatest military challenge so far in the form of an army led by the Anglo-Norman Earl of Ulster, Richard de Burgh. He was the most powerful of the English robber barons in Ireland. He was also a relative of Edward's by marriage; Robert the Bruce was married to de Burgh's daughter, Margaret.

King Edward II's administrator in Ireland, Edmund Butler, was also marching north with an army to fight the Scots, but when he met with de Burgh's force at Ardee it was agreed the Earl could defeat the invaders without Butler's help. De Burgh had no intention of letting the English king or his administrators meddle in what he regarded as a private war against the Bruces. De Burgh made an alliance with one of the most powerful of the native Gaelic leaders, 21-year-old Felim O'Connor of Connacht. However, Edward was in secret contact with O'Connor and persuaded him to desert the English cause. Unfortunately, Edward proved himself too sly for his own good and also made a deal supporting one of

O'Connor's rivals for power in Connacht. Backing both sides warring for control of Connacht did not encourage many of the Irish to trust Edward.

Edward may not have been as savvy a politician as his big brother, but his years of fighting the English had made him a formidable foe in battle. In September he tricked de Burgh into mistaking the Scottish baggage train for his main army and launching an attack on it near present-day Ballymena; Edward's troops then rushed down on de Burgh's army from behind and scattered it. Edward celebrated his latest triumph by devastating the Meath town of Nobber before continuing his march towards Dublin.

The next Englishman to face Edward was Roger Mortimer. He had been sent to Ireland by King Edward II, who wanted him out of the way for much the same reasons that led Robert the Bruce to dispatch his brother there. Both men were dangerous in their own countries. Mortimer would stage a coup against Edward II when he got back from Ireland which resulted in the king's death.

The Scots beat Mortimer at Kells in December 1315. Treachery again played a part in the victory and this time the traitors were Anglo-Norman. Mortimer had been acquiring power and land in Ireland at the expense of the de Lacy family. He should not have been surprised when they switched sides at Kells and joined the Scots.

Meanwhile, all hope of further help for the Scots from Felim O'Connor was extinguished when he was defeated and killed by the Anglo-Normans under Richard de Bermingham and de Burgh's brother, William. The English had helped O'Connor defeat his rival for the kingship of Connacht but then the Irishman had foolishly turned on his allies and attacked them. The alliance between O'Connor and de Bermingham must have been a strained one because de Bermingham's father, Piers, had organised the murder of 32 of the main O'Connor chieftains during a Christmas feast in 1295.

The Scots had meanwhile defeated Edmund Butler and his

army at Skerries in February 1316 and the road to Dublin now lay open. But Edward feared the English holed up at Carrickfergus were about to be reinforced from the sea and would emerge to attack him from behind so the Scots army turned away from Dublin and headed back to Carrickfergus. A shortage of food and horse fodder in the area surrounding Dublin due to the famine may also have played a part in Edward's decision to return north. The English garrison at Carrickfergus was eventually starved out in September 1316.

At some point Edward had himself crowned high king of Ireland at Faughart. But it was an empty gesture and few Irishmen recognised them as their sovereign. Even O'Neill's support was becoming increasingly lukewarm. Edward further failed to endear himself to his subjects when he celebrated his coronation by having several of them hanged.

Back in Scotland, Robert the Bruce realised the campaign in Ireland was faltering and he decided to intervene personally. In late 1316 he landed in Ireland with a force of heavily armed warriors recruited from the Western Isles and in February of the following year the Bruce brothers were marching on Dublin.

De Burgh tried to ambush the Scots en route to Dublin. The Scots were split into two columns; the lead one was commanded by Edward and was allowed through the ambush, but two English archers emerged from cover too soon and Robert was able to route the de Burgh's troops. De Burgh fled to Dublin. His link to the Bruces by marriage made him politically suspect to the English in Dublin and they threw him in jail. Mortimer later had him released.

The English also built a new defensive wall to protect the city and torched one of the suburbs to prevent it being used to house the besieging Scots. But the Bruces's army did not linger long near Dublin; without catapults and other siege engines, the Scots had little chance of capturing the city and they retreated back north to de Burgh's old lands. Robert the Bruce had probably seen for himself that his arrogant brother had little chance of being accepted as high king of Ireland and soon headed back to Scotland.

Mortimer, meanwhile, had decided to deal with the de Lacys before defeating Edward and what was left of the Scottish army in Ireland. The de Lacys were rounded up and their leader, John de Lacy, was crushed to death at Trim under a wooden door piled high with rocks.

Edward's days as a king were definitely numbered when the English regained control of the sea route between Scotland and Ireland and cut him off from all hope of further supplies or reinforcements from home. The supply situation for the Scots was becoming critical, because the Irish saw no point in planting crops which would only be stolen or destroyed by the competing armies marauding around the country.

Finally, in October 1318, an English army commanded by John de Bermingham was sent north to end Edward's royal pretensions. He decided to make his last stand near the site of his coronation at Faughart. O'Neill and the handful of Irish chieftains who still stood by Edward advised him the time had come to quit Ireland, but the proud Scot insisted on making a fight of it.

The two armies which met at Faughart on 14 October probably did not number more than 1,500 men each. Legend has it that de Bermingham donned a disguise to sneak into a pre-battle mass that Edward was attending so he would recognise the Scot on the battlefield and even spoke a few words to him. Several English knights had vowed to kill Edward and another legend maintains that he switched armour with one of his men, Gib Harper, to fool them. In view of Edward's well-known exaggerated sense of chivalry this latter legend sounds unlikely.

De Bermingham opened the battle by bringing his archers forward to unleash a hail of arrows into the Scots drawn up on the southern slopes of Faughart Hill. The Scots pulled back over the ridge of the hill to escape the arrows and waited for the inevitable charge by the heavily armoured English knights on their war horses. When the English topped the ridge, they found the Scots waiting for them in perfect order and in the fighting which followed Edward's men seemed to be getting the better of the contest. It even looked as though the Scots might win, but the balance tipped against them when Edward was killed. The fight went out of the Scots with their leader's death and it was all most could do to run for their lives.

The circumstances of Edward's death are unclear. Perhaps one of the Englishman who vowed to kill Edward did catch up with him, but there is another more intriguing version. It maintains that the Scots actually drove the English off Faughart Hill and Edward and some of his followers had stopped to catch their breath when an English assassin posing as a village idiot came capering up. The mentally handicapped were regarded as figures of fun and ridicule in those days and no doubt the man dressed in straw was encouraged in his lunatic cavorting by the mocking laughter of the battle-weary Scots. No-one appears to have been worried by the metal ball dangling on a chain around the idiot's waist. As he danced around close to Edward, he suddenly swung the ball and crushed the self-proclaimed high king of Ireland's head like a ripe melon. The other Scots cut the assassin down, but the battle was lost. The English cavalry had been hiding out of sight and now, at a pre-arranged signal, thundered forward to route the demoralised Scots.

Edward's body was found on the battlefield and his head was hacked off for public display. Accounts disagree on where the head was displayed; some say it only got as far as Dublin, others that it made it all the way to London. Or maybe it was Gib Harper's head that went on show? Both Irish and English chroniclers agree on one thing – Edward's invasion was a disaster for Ireland.

Then again, history is always written by, and for, the winners.

THE LOSER

VERNEUIL 1424

Archibald, 4th Earl of Douglas, really earned the nickname *Tineman*. In Scots, this means 'loser' and Archibald had a habit of losing battles and body parts on a regular basis. In two of the most disastrous battles in Scottish history he lost an eye and a testicle and his death on a French battlefield probably saved him from losing his head for the suspected murder of the heir to the Scottish throne in 1402.

Archibald was born in 1369 into one of the most powerful families in Scotland. The 'Black' Douglases had risen steadily in power and wealth since they had helped Robert the Bruce kick the English out of Scotland in 1314. Bruce's right-hand man had been James Douglas, also known as The Good Sir James; the label may well have been ironic as Sir James delighted in massacring prisoners and today would quite possibly be diagnosed as a psychopath. Children on both sides of the border were told to go to sleep quietly or, 'The Black Douglas'll get ye'.

By the time Archibald, a grandson of The Good Sir James, was born, the Douglases had a stranglehold on power in southern Scotland. Their armies frequently raided into England where they clashed with troops led by their English alter-egos, the Percy family, Earls of Northumberland. When, in 1400, the English king, Henry IV, invaded Scotland, it was Archibald who held Edinburgh Castle against him. Henry was eventually forced by a lack of supplies to give up the siege and return to England. In retaliation for the English invasion, Archibald led a Scottish army of 10,000 men south in 1402 and pillaged England as far south as Durham. The Scottish invasion also fulfilled Scotland's obligations to its long time ally, France, which was at war with England.

The English army raised to repel the Scottish invasion was led by the Earl of Northumberland and his son and heir, Harry Hotspur. They decided that rather than chase the Scots south, they would wait for the Scots near the border and intercept them on their way home. Archibald and his men arrived in the area of Wooler, about 15 miles south of the border, to find an English army blocking the road north.

Hotspur had drawn his men up on Homildon Hill with his archers on either flank. When Archibald led his men in a charge at the English centre, the Englishmen fell back while the archers moved forward to catch the Scots in a murderous crossfire. It used to be said that English and Welsh bowmen carried 24 Scottish lives on their belts because that was how many arrows they had.

The Scots broke and ran and Archibald was left behind with an arrow in one eye and four or five more through his plate armour. He was taken prisoner. The defeat cost 1,200 Scots their lives, including 500 or so who drowned in the River Tweed trying to get back home. However, Archibald and Hotspur must have hit it off, because the Scot joined the Englishman in his rebellion against Henry IV whilst still a prisoner. Much of the bitterness between the northern English noble and the king centred on who was entitled to the ransom money for Archibald and the other Scottish lords captured at Homildon.

The rebel and royal armies clashed at Shrewsbury and at first it looked as though Hotspur and Archibald might even win; but the pair could not resist the call of personal glory over good generalship and insisted on plunging into the thick of the battle. Together with a party of picked knights, they charged the spot on the battlefield where Henry IV's personal flag was seen flying.

Archibald cut down two men wearing the king's personal

insignia but neither was Henry IV. He had dressed up several men to resemble himself and both Hotspur and Douglas failed to find him in the scrum of armoured knights hacking at each other around the royal standard. Hotspur lifted the visor of his helmet to get a better view and was killed instantly by an arrow in the eye. His troops immediately lost heart and fled. Once again Archibald was left behind and became a prisoner, this time of Henry IV. His wounds included a missing testicle. He would remain a prisoner of the English until a substantial ransom was paid four or five years later.

The man reputed to have suggested to Henry IV that he should have several decoys with him at Shrewsbury was the renegade Scottish Earl of Dunbar. He knew Archibald would be unable to resist charging at Henry. Dunbar had a personal grudge against Archibald. He had hoped to marry his daughter to the heir to the throne, David, Duke of Rothesay but Rothesay had gone back on the deal when the Douglases offered a bigger dowry if he married Archibald's sister Marjorie instead. Dunbar left Scotland in disgust and his land was given to the Douglases. Archibald married Rothesay's sister Margaret, but he was still implicated in the duke's death at Falkland Palace, where the heir to the throne was being held prisoner by his uncle, the Duke of Albany.

The Scottish king had been christened John and took the name King Robert III at his coronation in 1390, probably because the name John would have had associations with John Balliol, the Toom Tabard. However, Robert III was a weak character and being kicked in the head by a horse had not improved his ability to govern; the real power in Scotland was in the hands of his younger brother, Robert, Duke of Albany. Albany ran Scotland, supported in the south of the country by the Douglases and in the north by his nephew, Alexander, Earl of Buchan.

In 1399 an assembly of the Scottish nobility made Rothesay 'Lieutenant of the Realm' in a bid to shift power out of Albany's hands; but Rothesay was an indecisive man and he failed to grab the chance he was being given. Within three years Albany and

Archibald felt strong enough to imprison Rothesay in Falkland Palace where he soon died; Albany and Archibald maintained that Rothesay died from natural causes, but it was widely believed he had been starved to death.

The heir to the throne now became Rothesay's brother James and Robert III decided to send him to France for safety but his ship was captured by English pirates in 1406 who handed the young heir over to Henry IV. When Henry died, he was succeeded by his son Henry V who decided to push his family's longstanding claim to the French throne. His main opposition came from the Dauphin, heir to the French throne and the effective ruler because his father was mad. The Scots honoured their treaty obligations to the French by sending troops to fight the English. Some Scots also fought for the English and Henry V took James, still a prisoner, on his campaign against the French.

In 1421 the English suffered a major setback when Henry V's brother, the Duke of Clarence, attacked the Scots army near Baugé while they were playing football. His failure to wait for his archers to arrive before attacking cost Clarence and 2,000 of his men their lives when they were cut to pieces by a ferocious Scots counter-charge led by Archibald's son, also called Archibald.

Meanwhile, Albany had little interest in seeing his nephew James released from English custody and it took several more years for his £40,000 ransom to be paid. James finally returned to Scotland in April 1424 to be crowned James I a month later. By that time Albany had been dead for four years, but his son Murdoch had taken over the running of the country. James had Murdoch and Murdoch's son Walter arrested and executed. We will never know whether he intended a similar fate for Archibald, who was already marching towards his final battle. Archibald was in France with 6,500 men to fight for the Dauphin. This meant going back on a deal he had made to hire out 200 knights and the same number of mounted archers to the English for £200.

Archibald was given command of a joint Scottish-French army numbering around 14,000 men and on 17 August 17 1424 he clashed with an English army commanded by Henry V's uncle, the Duke of Bedford. Sadly for the Scots, they had made it known that the battle was going to be a fight to the death and no prisoners would be taken. The English took them at their word and few Scots were to survive the encounter.

Archibald drew his dismounted men-at-arms up into two wings, one Scots and one French, and placed his cavalry on either flank. The English also formed up into two wings, one commanded by Bedford and the other by the Earl of Salisbury. The English had about 1,000 archers guarding their baggage train in the rear.

The battle started well for Archibald. His cavalry on the left wing brushed past the English and routed the archers guarding the baggage. But then they lost interest in the battle and began looting the baggage. Archibald's Italian mercenary cavalry rode round from their position on the right wing and joined in the looting without even fighting any Englishmen.

Bedford's men found themselves locked in a slogging match with the French while Salisbury was pushed back by the Scots. Then the French suddenly broke and ran. Bedford was able to advance and then swing round to attack the Scots from behind. The Scots were surrounded and had nowhere to run. It was a massacre as Archibald and the flower of the Scottish nobility accompanying him were slaughtered.

Only 200 Scots lived to be taken prisoner. Some others managed to break out of the encircling English horde and rejoin the French army. The Dauphin was so impressed by them that the Scots became his personal bodyguard and Scottish troops remained part of the regular French army until 1789. The Royal Scots claimed descent from a regiment once in French service under the name Le Regiment De Douglas. Not all Frenchmen were sad to see the Scots pretty much wiped out at Verneuil; many Frenchmen looked on the Scots as nothing more than wine-guzzling, mutton-chomping savages.

The total Dauphinist losses at battle have been estimated in the region of 7,000 men. The English lost about 1,600 men. The Scots would never again make a significant contribution to what has gone down in history as the One Hundred Years War, the period of conflict between the French and English from 1337 to 1453. Between 1419 and 1424 an estimated 15,000 Scots, two percent of the population, fought in France and perhaps as many as half of them died there. Archibald, who had been made Constable of France before his death, was buried at Tours Cathedral.

His son Archibald became 5th Earl and it was another 60 years, filled with murder and intrigue, before the Stewart dynasty finally broke the grip that the Black Douglases had on power in Scotland.

RENAISSANCE MAN

FLODDEN 1513

King James IV is regarded as one of Scotland's best monarchs. He brought his troublesome nobles under control and was a patron of the arts and sciences. But he was also a Stewart and he led Scots troops to one of the country's worst defeats – and against a heavily outnumbered English army at that.

To describe the Stewarts as trouble-prone verges on understatement. James IV's father and great-grandfather were murdered by the Scots nobles, his grand-daughter, Mary Queen of Scots, was beheaded for plotting against her cousin, Elizabeth I of England, and his great-great grandson Charles I was executed by the English Parliament for his part in plunging Britain into two bloody civil wars.

James came to the throne in 1488 after his father was defeated by an army of rebel Scottish nobles at the Battle of Sauchieburn and then murdered as he lay wounded in a mill near the battlefield. James was 15 years old at the time of the murder and always blamed himself for his weakness in being seen to encourage the nobles in their rebellion and the murder of his father. In penance, he wore an iron chain around his waist for the rest of his life.

James matured into a true Renaissance prince; he was intelligent and high spirited. We will never know which of these two characteristics led him to encourage early scientist John Damian in his belief in manned flight; Damian's dream came to an abrupt end when he plunged to his death from the ramparts of Stirling Castle in a bid to prove he could indeed fly. James also dabbled in dentistry and pulled several of his barber's teeth to satisfy his curiosity about the science. He also established Britain's first medical school, at King's College in Aberdeen, and forced his nobles to send their children to school. In 1491 he banned the playing of football in Scotland but then ignored his own law six years later by buying footballs for his own use.

But James was also a notorious womaniser. The Scots nobles poisoned the porridge of one of his mistresses, Margaret Drummond, and her two sisters in a bid to persuade him that the time had come to do his dynastic and diplomatic duty by marrying the daughter of the English king, Henry VII. He married Margaret Tudor in 1502 and the marriage was judged a success. James, though, refused to completely abandon his womanizing ways and fathered several illegitimate children.

James's biggest problem was that he had pretensions beyond what his pitifully poor realm justified. He believed he was one of the great kings of Europe and should have a large part to play in its affairs both as a kingmaker and peace-broker. When Henry VII died, James quickly found himself at loggerheads with his brother-in-law, the new king of England, Henry VIII.

Henry also had pretensions as a European power-broker and it was not long before he invaded Scotland's traditional ally, France; James took the side of the French against 'The Auld Enemy'. The French immediately sent money and arms to their Scottish allies. In a move intended to exploit James's vanity and sense of Renaissance romance, the queen of France sent him a turquoise ring and an appeal to him to act as her knightly champion against the English.

The instrument of James's victory over the English was to be a massive Scots army armed with 18-foot pikes and drilled to fight in tightly packed columns. The battlefields of Europe were dominated at the time by Swiss and German mercenaries who swept away all opposition with their pike columns. The problem was that for a pike column attack to succeed, it had to be conducted by highly trained and experienced men with a clear run at the enemy. When James's invading army met the English at Flodden in 1513, it had neither.

The army James led was the biggest ever raised in Scotland up to that time; every community in the country was ordered to provide men for it and soon Edinburgh was overflowing with ruddy-faced youths champing at the bit to do battle with the hated English. The French sent instructors to teach the Scots how to use the 18-foot pikes issued to them and impart all the latest tactics being used on the Continent.

Most of the pikemen wore iron skull caps and canvas jackets with metal plates sewn on as primitive armour; they also carried small wooden shields. The front ranks of each pike column were made up of nobles and minor gentry wearing heavy plate armour, much of it the latest arrow-proof design from European workshops, and carrying large rectangular wooden shields. The soldiers from the Highlands were more lightly armoured. Some had no armour at all while others wore only long chainmail shirts. They preferred two-handed broadswords and bows as weapons rather than the pikes issued to the Lowlanders.

By the time James was ready to invade, he had perhaps as many as 60,000 men with him. The cream of the English chivalry and most of the country's available manpower had gone with Henry VIII to France. Henry had left the northern counties of England untouched by his levy of troops to fight in France, but the available pool of men available to repel a Scots invasion numbered no more than 30,000. They were armed mainly with bows and arrows or bills. The bill, an axe head and hook on the end of an eight-foot pole, was already regarded as an obsolete weapon in the rest of Europe.

It must have looked to James like the best chance the Scots had ever had of successfully invading northern England. But in Scotland, ghostly apparitions and other supernatural occurrences were being reported. All warned against going ahead with the invasion. A mysterious man in a blue robe and sandals was said to have appeared to James at a church service in Linlithgow and, in front of dozens of witnesses, warned him of a major disaster ahead. The mystery man then vanished into thin air.

At first the invasion appeared to be going well. Several castles in Northumberland were besieged and captured using the heavy artillery guns James brought with him. Just before the clash at Flodden, the Scottish Parliament met for the first and only time on English soil. It passed an act exempting the families of those killed in the fighting from paying death duties. Few could have realised just how many families would benefit from the new law.

Eventually, the English army under the 73-year-old Earl of Surrey, Thomas Howard, arrived in Northumberland and a showdown loomed. James and his army took up a strong position on a ridge at Flodden, about seven miles from the border. The gently rolling border landscape seemed perfectly suited to James's pike column tactics.

The wily Howard knew his 26,000-strong army stood little chance of success in a direct attack on the Scots drawn up on the ridge at Flodden; some local men told him of a route that would take the English army north around the Scots position and place it near the border. Howard knew the Scots would be forced to leave their positions to deal with the threat posed by an English army north of them. About one-third of James's army had already deserted and gone back to Scotland and the sight of English troops blocking the way home could only increase the rate of desertion. Some Scots were convinced that the road was open for the English to march in to Scotland unopposed and put the country to fire and sword.

An exchange of heralds led to a date being set for battle – 9 September. It was typical of James to agree to such chivalrous behaviour as tying himself to a date; his nobles all agreed that the king needed to be kept on a tight leash because his romantic instincts could easily lead to the kind of brave and chivalrous attack which would cost the Scots dearly.

On the morning of the day of battle, the English were seen

heading for Branxton Hill, a mile north of the Scottish positions. Branxton Hill was not as strong a defensive position as Flodden, but it was still a good one. The Scots set off for Branxton Hill as well and managed to reach it first. The English formed up on a lower ridge just north of the hill.

Although they'd lost the race, the new English position on the lower ridge offered them two advantages. Artillery technology at the time meant firing downhill was a tricky business but firing uphill was easy. More importantly, there was a bog in the small valley between the two armies which the Scots would have to negotiate before beginning the climb up to the English positions. Going through the bog would cost the Scots much of the momentum that a tightly packed pike column needed to smash the enemy.

The wise thing for James to have done would have been to pull his men back behind the crest of Branxton Hill out of English artillery range and wait for the English to attack him. Instead, the Scots stayed where they were and an artillery duel began around 4pm. The English gunners, more experienced and with the advantage of firing uphill, easily got the better of it and English cannon balls were soon tearing into the ranks of tightly packed Scots.

Perhaps unable to stand the artillery fire any more, the 10,000 Scottish borderers and Highlanders under the command of Lord Home on the left wing of James's army, suddenly erupted into a charge. The charge swept away the English levies in its path but then things started to go wrong. Instead of swinging around and attacking the English centre from the flank, the Scots started looting the bodies of the English dead. The English border lancers who made up Howard's cavalry charged the Scots and drove them back towards Branxton Hill.

By this time, James and his pike columns were moving down the slopes of Branxton Hill to attack the English centre. It is possible James believed that Home and his men would indeed launch a flank attack on the centre and wanted to take advantage of it. The battlefield went quiet and all that could be heard was the clanking of the Scots' armour as the columns of pikemen tramped down the hill.

But as could have been predicted, the Scots ran into trouble when they reached the boggy dip at the foot of the hill and the columns started to lose their momentum. The obsolete bills carried by the English now came into their own. They hacked the steel heads off the Scottish pikes and turned them into useless sticks. When the Scots threw the pikes aside and drew their swords, they found the eight-foot shafts on the bills gave the English the reach advantage, although it still took six or seven blows with a bill to fell the heavily armoured Scots in the front ranks of the pike columns. The battle in the centre saw the two sides locked in a bloody hacking and shoving match on the edge of the bog. Perhaps sheer weight of numbers might have given the Scots victory but a brilliant English attack on the right flank clinched the battle for them.

For some reason the Highlanders who made up the right wing of James's army had not joined the attack. An English force under Sir Edward Stanley managed to sneak up on the Highlanders and take them by surprise from the flank and rear. The Highlanders fled and Stanley's men turned to run back down Branxton Hill into the rear of James's columns fighting in the centre. To have any chance of success, the pike columns had to keep moving, but the attack from behind brought the slow push against the English centre grinding to a halt.

The Scots, with their unwieldy 18-foot pikes, were unable to turn to meet the new threat. Soon the English were closing in from all sides. It was a slaughter. The English had no intention of letting any Scots trapped within their ring of slashing steel escape alive.

James, fighting on foot, led a desperate charge deep into the English centre but he and his men were soon cut off from the rest of the Scots throng and hacked to pieces. When his body was pulled from the bottom of a bloody pile of Scots corpses next morning, he had several arrow wounds and his head was attached to his body by only a shred of skin. The two-hour battle had costs thousands of Scottish lives, including more than a dozen earls. Estimates of the number of Scottish dead vary between 5,000 and 15,000. The English are generally agreed to have lost 1,500 men.

The slaughter of Scotland's brightest and best was not to be repeated on such a scale again until the First World War. It was not uncommon for a community that sent 50 men to fight for James to have only one blood-stained ragged survivor come home again. One of the oldest Scots to die was 90-year-old William Maitland from Lethington.

News of the defeat at Flodden had the citizens of Edinburgh scurrying to build a new defensive wall, but Howard knew he did not have enough men to invade Scotland. The expected invasion never came and James's 17-month old son, James V, was crowned without any English interference. A special miniature crown was made for the coronation.

James's body was cleaned and embalmed before being sent to London where it was thrown in a storeroom like a piece of rubbish. Years later English workmen played football with his head after finding it, still red-haired and bearded, in a London woodshed. The head was later buried in an unmarked grave in a London churchyard.

It was hardly the treatment a man who regarded himself as one of the premier princes of Christendom would have expected.

MASSACRE IN NORWAY

KRINGEN 1612

The ambush and massacre of a party of Scottish mercenaries in 1612 proved a key historical event for Norwegian nationalists trying to foster an independence movement from Sweden in the early 19th century. The myth-makers fastened onto the so-called Battle of Kringen as an example of gallant Norwegians banding together to repel a foreign foe. The fact that many of the 134 Scots murdered after the ambush had been virtually kidnapped and forced into mercenary service appears to have been conveniently forgotten.

But what were the Scots doing in Norway in 1612 anyway?

The answer lies in a power battle for control of the reputed mineral wealth of sparsely populated northern Norway and the rich fishing grounds off its shores. Norway was ruled at the time by Denmark, but Sweden claimed ownership of the northern part of the country. Even if the reports of mineral wealth proved false, the tolls levied on English and Dutch fishing boats operating off the North Cape would provide much needed income to whoever controlled the area. Russia was also making ownership claims in the region.

The dispute between Denmark and Sweden boiled over into open warfare in 1611 and only ended with a Danish victory in 1613.

Mercenaries were a major part of any European king's army in those days and the war between Denmark and Sweden proved no exception. Amsterdam was the main mercenary recruiting base for northern Europe and that is where the Swedes headed looking for soldiers. Scotland was always a reliable source of mercenaries and there were several Scots based in Amsterdam who were prepared to provide soldiers of fortune to anyone for the right money. One of them, Sir James Spens, quickly recruited a force of 3,000 men for the Swedes and landed them at Gothenburg in April 1612; but the mercenaries were captured when the city and its fortress fell to the Danes shortly afterwards.

However, there were plenty more Scots available to fight for the Swedes. Scotland was a poor nation and the lawless Borders and Highlands were both areas of almost continual fighting; there were many Scots around who knew how to handle a sword or firearm. This time the recruiting was put in the hands of veteran mercenaries Jan Van Monkhoven and Andrew Ramsay. Half the new force was to be recruited in mainland Europe by Van Monkhoven while Ramsay brought the remainder across from Scotland. But it was not only the Swedes who had agents in Amsterdam; the Danes were watching Ramsay closely and intercepted him almost as soon as he set sail for Scotland. The Scot was forced to promise he would forget all about his contract with the Swedes before the Danes released him.

Ramsay gave his word, but he did not intend to keep it. As soon as he got back to Scotland he began recruiting. He had men scouring the country and he did not care where his soldiers came from or whether they were volunteers or not. There were complaints lodged with the Scottish authorities that Ramsay's men had been taking 'honest men's bairns and servants' and keeping them as 'slaves and captives'. The jails at Dunbar and Edinburgh were visited by the mercenary recruiters, who told the men that agreeing to serve King Charles IX of Sweden would mean freedom after the fighting was over.

Ramsay shrugged off all attempts by the Scottish authorities to intervene in his recruiting drive by claiming it was backed by James I and the royal court in London. No-one seems to have wondered why the king, who as James VI of Scotland had inherited the

English crown in 1603, would be backing the Swedes against his brother-in-law King Christian IV of Denmark.

It is possible that James, who was a great admirer of Ramsay's, turned a blind eye to the recruitment drive until he was forced to act by official complaints about it from the Danes. James then told the Scottish Privy Council, which ran the country on his behalf, to halt the recruiting drive and arrest Ramsay. He claimed to be baffled to find his privy councillors had allowed the recruitment drive and put their lack of action down to incompetence.

Ramsay had meanwhile gone on the run, but he was captured after coming out of hiding to challenge Sir Robert Ker, the man he believed had betrayed his scheme to James, to a duel; Ramsay got off with banishment. Several ships containing Ramsay's mercenaries that had been anchored in the Firth of Forth were ordered to put their human cargo back ashore. However, the Privy Council failed to do anything about a shipload of mercenaries which was allowed to sail out of Dundee under the command of Ramsay's brother Alexander.

It rendezvoused with a ship containing a party of hardened mercenaries recruited in Caithness by George Sinclair, a nephew of the 5th Earl of Caithness. The two ships arrived in a fjord near Romsdal in Norway on 19 August, where they landed a force of about 300 Scots for a cross-country march to Sweden. The loss of the Elfsborg fortress at Gothenburg had closed off sea access to Sweden for the Scots, but the mercenary leaders did not anticipate that the march was dangerous because the Norwegians were believed to be lukewarm in their support for the Danes.

The 100 or so men who sailed from Dundee were put at the head of the column and treated more like prisoners than comrades in arms by Sinclair's men. The Dundee men likely included many of the 'bairns and servants' forced to become mercenaries by Ramsay's recruiters. The march got off to a bad start when the guide the Scots recruited, local farmer Peder Klognaes, managed to add a gruelling 14 extra miles to the route on the first day; his navigation got better after he was dangled by his heels off a bridge by a party of angry mercenaries.

The mercenaries had misread the temper and loyalty of the Norwegians. As the Scots marched on, a steadily growing force of Norwegian peasant militia was retreating ahead of them. Several votes were taken over the days following the Scots landing on whether to fight the invaders, but on each occasion the majority opinion was in favour of continued retreat. On the seventh day, when the Scots were over 150 miles into their march, it was decided the time had come for a showdown.

An ambush site was selected near the town of Kringen, where steep wooded cliffs reduced the road alongside the fast running River Laugen to a single-file track. The Norwegian commander, local magistrate Lauritz Hage, had about 400 men under his command by the time it was decided to fight. Many Norwegians had drifted away after the Scots marched past their communities and left them unmolested, but they were replaced by fresh militiamen from settlements further east.

Boulders were piled up on the cliffs ready to be rolled down onto the road when the right time came. The plan was to use the boulders to close both ends of the narrow pass and then unleash a second avalanche onto the Scots trapped below. The Norwegians allowed the poorly armed Dundee contingent through the pass before springing the ambush. Local legend has it that the signal that the Scots were approaching the trap was given by a local girl called Prillar Guri on her lur horn.

Some Norwegians opened fire with their muskets before the rocks came tumbling down on the Scots. The marksmen were too far away to hit the Scots and they responded with contemptuous jeers and catcalls. The firing may have distracted the Scots long enough to stop them spotting the rocks poised to come down on top of them until it was too late. Once Sinclair and his men were strung out along the narrow track beside the river, the rocks were unleashed and their escape was blocked. More rocks were now rolled down on the Scots and Norwegian marksmen began shooting again.

A militiaman called Berdon Sejelstad had equipped himself

with a silver bullet especially to kill Sinclair, who was widely believed by the Norwegians to be an agent of Satan. Sejelstad did not miss and Sinclair was one of the first Scots killed. His wife and baby soon followed him. The baby was first to die and when a Norwegian tried to lead the distraught woman to safety, she stabbed him to death. The Norwegian's comrades then shot Sinclair's wife dead.

For almost 90 minutes the trapped Scots were pelted with rocks and shot at. Those who tried to swim the river were drowned or killed by Norwegian peasants lurking on the far bank. The Scots could make little reply because their firearms had been confiscated in Scotland and the Norwegians were smart enough to keep out of reach of their axes and swords. Still, the Scots managed to kill six Norwegians and wound a dozen more.

When the Norwegians finally called a halt to the slaughter, only 134 of the 300 Scots were still standing. Most of them were from the Dundee contingent which had surrendered early on without much of a fight.

Alexander Ramsay, as nominal head of the expedition, had been at the head of the column with the Dundee men and was taken prisoner along with another officer called Henry Bruce. Along with the mercenaries' translator, James Moneypenny, and a servant called James Scott, the two officers were sent away for questioning by the Danish authorities. The men downplayed their roles in the expedition and claimed Sinclair was their leader. They added they had no idea they were being asked to fight the Danes and said they believed they had been recruited for a war against Russia. Their excuses were accepted and all four were released.

A dozen or so of the men they left behind at Kringen managed to save their lives by volunteering their services as mercenaries in the Danish army or agreeing to work on local farms. The Norwegians celebrated their victory with a night of partying at which it was agreed they would kill their remaining 116 prisoners. Two-by-two the Scots were led from the barn where they were being held captive and shot dead. When a Danish board of inquiry demanded to know the reason for the murders, no-one could give a satisfactory explanation.

The Danish Crown commissioners who investigated the massacre found that the Scots had gone out of their way not to antagonise the Norwegians during their march. However, the activities of the 800 men commanded by Van Monkhoven when they marched across Norway in July 1612 may offer a clue to the Norwegians' actions. Van Monkhoven's men raped and pillaged all along the route of their march. The Swedes had also raised the ire of the Norwegians by massacring 300 of their countrymen captured just north of Gothenburg. Many of the murdered Norwegians came from the Romsdal and Kringen areas.

The ambush and massacre of the Scots soon became the stuff of legend for the Norwegians. In the 19th century, nationalists, now seeking independence from Sweden, seized on the episode as an example of Norwegian courage, cunning and love of freedom. Killing prisoners of war, many of them kidnapped from their homes by ruthless mercenary recruiters and never expecting to fight people who were under Danish occupation, is shamefully sordid.

Nevertheless, it is from such events that nationalistic myths are woven.

THE DEATH MARCH

DUNBAR 1650

With the odds apparently two-to-one in their favour, the young Scots camped on a hill overlooking Dunbar in the autumn of 1650 felt confident of victory over the English invader. But instead the English commander Oliver Cromwell inflicted a humiliating defeat on the Scots and doomed thousands of them to die as his prisoners.

Cromwell declared his victory at Dunbar as the greatest of his career. It is perhaps ironic that his previous greatest victory, against Charles I at Marston Moor in 1644, had been won for him by the Scots. However, the Puritans who dominated the English Parliament fell foul of their Scots allies by executing Charles I; the Scots had handed the king over to the English Parliament in 1647 on condition that no harm would befall him. The English had also broken their agreement to impose a Scottish-style Presbyterian church system on their fellow countrymen.

The Scots reacted by declaring Charles's son their king, as Charles II, and Cromwell was sent north in July 1650 to crush the new Royalist menace. The Scots army was commanded by General David Leslie, an experienced veteran of the bitter religious wars that had been raging throughout mainland Europe for decades. He opted for a scorched-earth policy which saw the Scots retreat in the face of the English invaders, destroying all the food and fuel they could not carry away.

This forced Cromwell to stick close to the coast route between

Berwick-on-Tweed and Edinburgh to ensure his army could be supplied by the English navy. As he approached Edinburgh, Cromwell found the Scots occupying a series of strongly held positions which blocked his path. Leslie was one step ahead of Cromwell all the way and every time the English tried a new route to the city, they found the Scots waiting for them in some impregnable position. After six weeks of futile campaigning, the English army of 16,000 men had been reduced by sickness to nearer 11,000. Then they found that Leslie had cut off their retreat back to England and trapped them at the coastal town of Dunbar.

Although the Scots with 22,000 men now outnumbered the English by two-to-one, they weren't without their own problems. The Presbyterian zealots who dominated Scottish politics had forced Leslie to dismiss almost 100 of his best and most experienced officers because they were regarded as politically suspect or not religious enough. Another 3,000 of his men had been sent home for failing to live up to the high moral standards of behaviour imposed upon them. The Scottish army had been formed by a levy that demanded communities from across Lowland Scotland give up a specified quota of men in their teens or early twenties for military service. One disillusioned officer said of his colleagues that too many were, 'ministers' sons, clerks and other sanctified creatures, who hardly ever heard of a sword but that of the Spirit.'

Leslie had occupied an almost impregnable position overlooking Dunbar on Doon Hill. But while Cromwell could not attack Leslie as long as he remained on Doon Hill, Leslie could not get at Cromwell's troops either. There were fears that if Leslie did not make a move soon, the English fleet would have time to evacuate Cromwell's men from Dunbar. Popular legend has it that the same Presbyterian ministers who purged the Scots army of its best troops, also ordered Leslie down off Doon Hill. Another source suggests that the Covenanters amongst Leslie's forces refused to fight on the Sabbath and forced Leslie to delay. Whatever the reason, it appears it was Leslie himself who decided to break the stalemate and move in to finish off Cromwell's army as quickly as possible. Also, the miserable Scottish weather which had played so much havoc on Cromwell's army was also taking a toll on the Scots; the troops camped high on Doon Hill were constantly buffeted by wind and rain.

As it turned out, Cromwell had no plans for a sea evacuation, but he knew it would take a miracle to save his army. Leslie handed him that miracle on a plate. When the Scots descended from Doon Hill they positioned themselves for an attack on the English camp next morning, 3 September. The last thing Leslie expected was that Cromwell would attack him first.

But while the Scots were perfectly poised for an attack, the positions they took up made them vulnerable in defence. The Scots were crammed in a three-mile line along a narrow strip of land between the foot of Doon Hill and a boggy stream called the Brox Burn with left little room for manoeuvre. Cromwell decided to launch a surprise night attack on the right wing of the Scots army with a regiment of his best cavalry and three regiments of infantry. This involved a tricky night march and crossing the Brox Burn north of the Scottish positions. Night marches are always difficult military operations but Cromwell's seasoned and highly disciplined veterans accomplished the move without much difficulty.

The rest of his army was to launch a frontal attack across the Brox Burn and prevent the Scots soldiers on the left wing from reinforcing the right wing. By 4am Cromwell and his men were in position north of Scots, ready to sweep down on the right wing. The signal for the frontal attack was given and the battle began. The Scots were taken completely by surprise. Many were still asleep when the English attacked at dawn. Muskets were stacked and the burning fuses used to touch off the powder in them had been extinguished. The Scottish right flank quickly disintegrated into chaos. Some Scottish regiments fought back bravely, but Cromwell at the head of his heavy cavalry finally swept them away with a determined charge.

A force of English cavalry had crossed the Brox Burn south of the Scots and Leslie's men were now boxed in with Cromwell's troops attacking them from the north, south and east. The steep slopes of Doon Hill to the west made an orderly retreat impossible. Now the Scots' superior numbers told against them as their tightly packed regiments struggled to find enough room to manoeuvre.

The whole battle lasted less than an hour and quickly turned into a rout. It is not known how many of the 3,000 Scots killed were slain on the battlefield and how many were cut down by the English cavalry who chased them for eight miles towards Edinburgh. Cromwell reported to the English Parliament that he had only lost 30 men.

By the end of the day, the English had captured 10,000 Scots. Half of the prisoners were sent home immediately as too sick, weak or badly wounded to present any further military threat to the English; but between 4,500 and 5,000 Scots were marched south into England. The fate of the prisoners was a subject of much debate amongst the English leadership in London. Some wanted all the Scots officers and Presbyterian ministers captured at Dunbar executed. Another proposal involved murdering one-in-ten of the prisoners and selling the rest into bondage in America and the Caribbean. Both plans were rejected, but the journey south turned out to be a death march for the Scots. Prisoners who fell behind the straggling column were butchered on the spot by their English captors. It is not clear how many Scots managed to escape during the march but all who were recaptured were killed.

The Scots were starving by the time they reached Morpeth three days after the march had begun. Corralled in a farmer's field, the starving Scots gorged themselves on cabbage leaves and roots. For water, they drank from puddles and polluted roadside ditches. When they reached Newcastle, 500 of them were judged unfit to continue the march. They were housed in St Nicholas' Church where they died in droves as they lay amongst the pews.

When the column finally completed the 120-mile march to Durham on 11 September, only 3,000 Scots were still with it; they were to be imprisoned in the majestic Durham Cathedral. The Governor of Newcastle, Arthur Haselrigge, had been made responsible for the welfare of the prisoners and arranged for food and fuel to be supplied but corrupt guards and officials at Durham siphoned off nearly everything to sell to local merchants, meanwhile in the cramped cathedral, dysentery was raging amongst the starving Scots. By mid-October they were dying at a rate of up to 100 per day; desperate men fought and killed each other over scraps of food and warm clothing.

'Some were killed by themselves,' noted Haselrigge in a report to his superiors. 'For they are exceedingly cruel towards the other. If one man was perceived to have any money, it was two-to-one he was killed before morning and robbed. If any had good clothes that [a prisoner] wanted, he would strangle the other and put on his clothes. They were so unruly, sluttish and nasty that it is not to be believed. They acted like beasts rather than men.'

The Scots tore up the pews in the cathedral for fuel and broke open the tombs of local nobility buried there, looking for jewels they could trade for food from their corrupt guards. The bones of the long-dead were even burned for fuel. Around 100 of the fittest prisoners were sold into slavery down coal mines in north-east England or forced to do other dangerous work for their new masters. The English Parliament in London was bombarded with letters from English merchants who wanted a share of the lucrative contracts to ship the remaining prisoners across the Atlantic and sell them into bondage.

However, before the Scots could be shipped into slavery, the dysentery outbreak at the cathedral had to run its course. Haselrigge reported that 1,600 Scots died while being held there; their mass grave was found in the cathedral grounds in 1946. Eventually, 500 of the survivors were sold to the French army while another 900 were shipped across the Atlantic. It is not known how many died on the voyage, but a death rate of ten percent was not uncommon for an Atlantic crossing in those days. The figure was probably higher for the Scots who would have still been in poor health following their imprisonment at Durham.

Once they arrived at the English colonies in Virginia and

Massachusetts, life was hard for the young Scots. They had been sold into bondage for periods varying between six and eight years to local businessmen who used them for work no freeman would do. Many were sent to isolated camps in the backwoods to produce charcoal or cut timber.

The Scots sent to Barbados were even less fortunate. They were drafted for military service against the Spanish. The Caribbean at that time was a notoriously unhealthy place for Europeans and disease probably meant that few of the Scots saw their native land again.

The defeat of the Scots at Dunbar opened the way for a military occupation of Scotland which lasted until Cromwell died and the English, tired of military rule, restored Charles II to the throne in 1660.

THE BRAW LADS

NAMUR 1695

One minute, the men of the Edinburgh Regiment were attacking the French-held fortress at Namur and in the next moment the unit had almost ceased to exist. More than 500 members of the regiment were blown to pieces when the French detonated a stock of gunpowder under the feet of the Scots who were storming the ramparts of the Belgian fortress in August 1695. The attacking force was part of King William III's army that was attempting to drive the French out of the Low Countries and Namur would be William's final battle against the French. One of the strongest fortifications in Europe at the time and commanding the strategically important junction of the Meuse and Sambre rivers, it had a garrison of 16,000 crack French troops at the time of the siege. The Scots Guards and the Royal Scots had both played key roles in storming the town but the fortress held out.

The Edinburgh Regiment was then brought in to attack the crucial St Nicholas Gate into the fortress. What no-one realised was that the French had placed a mine packed with gunpowder near the gate which they set off as the Scots were about rush the key position. Despite their massive losses, the Scots pressed on with their attack and stormed onto the fortress wall. They held off French counter-attacks until reinforcements arrived. After further fighting, once again involving the Royal Scots, the French surrendered the fortress and sued for peace.

The regiment, raised only six years earlier, had gained its first battle of honour at Namur and was reformed; after several name changes, the regiment finally became the King's Own Scottish Borderers.

Namur was not the regiment's first battle. It had been raised in Edinburgh in only two hours in late March 1689 to help deal with a Highland uprising in support of James II.

It was one of only two regiments which did not disgrace itself in the face of a ferocious charge of broadsword-swinging Highlanders at the Battle of Killiecrankie in July 1689; the inexperienced youngsters of Lord Leven's Regiment (as the regiment was first known) and the English Hasting's Regiment were the only two units to hold their ground in the face of the Highland charge. The young Edinburgh men certainly did a better job than the hardened veterans of the Dutch army's Scotch Brigade at the battle; the Scottish mercenaries fled the Highlanders as fast as their legs would carry them.

The people of Edinburgh were so pleased with the way Leven's men behaved that they insisted they be renamed the Edinburgh Regiment. They further honoured the regiment by giving it the right to march through the city, fully armed with flags flying and drums beating, any time it liked without seeking the permission of the Lord Provost.

The death of the victorious Highlanders' commander at Killiecrankie, John Graham of Claverhouse, better known as Bonnie Dundee, took the wind out of the Stuart supporters' sails. A month later the gallant defence of Dunkeld by the Cameronians, outnumbered five-to-one, in a ferocious house-to-house battle broke the Highlanders' spirit. The Cameronians were another regiment hastily raised to fight for William III. It traced its roots to the armed men who had stood as armed guards at illegal Covenanter prayer meetings. Claverhouse had been in the forefront of trying to suppress the activities of preachers like Richard Cameron and his Covenanter followers, who became known as Cameronians. They knew Dundee only as 'Bluidy Clavers' for his savage part in trying to impose Episcopalianism on the Presbyterian Lowlands.

One reason for the government army's defeat by the Highlanders at Killiecrankie was that the redcoat troops had to plug their bayonets into the muzzles of their muskets. This prevented them from firing a final volley at close range into the charging Highlanders. Legend has it that the Scots-born commander of the government troops at Killiecrankie, General Hugh Mackay, introduced a new bayonet into British service as a result of the battle. It had a ring-like bracket which fitted over the musket's muzzle instead of into it. In reality, the socket bayonet's invention is credited to the French, although some sources say it was pioneered by the Swedes. The Edinburgh Regiment were amongst the first British troops to encounter the new style of bayonet.

In one of the battles leading up to the siege of Namur, the Scots came face to face with a French unit. When they saw the French fixing their bayonets, the Scots assumed the enemy were using the old-style type and would be unable to fire another volley. The Scots mounted their bayonets and charged. The surprise close-range volley from the French sent the Scots reeling but they managed to regain their momentum and throw the enemy back.

The bayonet, plug or socket, was a controversial weapon for the next 300 years. While many questioned its worth as a weapon, few soldiers doubted its worth in battle. Several commentators noted that while few men suffered bayonet wounds in battle, the sight alone of cold steel had won many a fight. During the Napoleonic wars, more than 100 years after Namur, one British surgeon noted: 'Opposing regiments when found in line and charging with fixed bayonets, never meet and struggle hand-to-hand and foot-to-foot, and this is for the best possible reason, that one side turns and runs as the other comes close enough to do mischief.'

The bayonet proved more of a psychological weapon than a physical one. There is something unnerving about a screaming man charging head on at you with the sole intent of impaling you on a piece of sharpened steel. Less than half a percent of British casualties in the First World War were caused by bayonet wounds but most armies today continue to issue their troops with bayonets. Bayonet training is still regarded as an excellent way of turning young men into killers and encouraging 'offensive spirit'. Most other things being equal, the more aggressive troops still usually win the fight.

THE AULD ENEMY

CULLODEN 1746

Sometimes popular memory is closer to the truth than professional historians will admit. To most people the Battle of Culloden in April 1746 is perceived as a fight between Scots and English. It was, in fact, not quite that simple; there were three Scottish infantry regiments fighting for 'The English' at Culloden and more Highlanders were involved in trying to crush the Jacobite Rebellion than actively supported it. Those facts are true, but what they hide is that while the Scots did not see Culloden as a Scotland v England conflict, the English most certainly did.

When Charles Edward Louis John Cazymyr Sylvester Severino Maria Stuart disembarked onto the shore at Borrodale in July 1745 to reclaim the British throne that his grandfather James II had thrown away 60 years earlier through bull-headed stupidity, he found the country in deep trouble.

England and Scotland had been ruled by a British Parliament since the 1707 Act of Union, but the English-dominated government paid little attention to either the letter or the spirit of the treaty. The English did not have to; in the House of Commons, English MPs outnumbered their Scottish counterparts 513 to 45 and in the House of Lords there were 196 English peers to 16 Scots. The treaty enshrined the preservation of the Scottish legal system but it did not take long before the English started tinkering with it. The House of Lords was declared the ultimate court of legal appeal despite the fact that it was dominated by English-trained lawyers. Treaty promises to preserve the rights of the Presbyterian Church in Scotland were ignored with equally casual disregard.

The Scots had been bullied into the union by promises that the economic warfare being waged against them by the English would end when the treaty was signed. In reality the union brought economic misery as local industries were destroyed by a flood of cheap goods from the south, while parliament passed laws which favoured English manufacturers at the expense of their Scots competitors.

The only Scottish city to benefit from the Treaty of Union was Glasgow, which flourished thanks to a lively trade with the English-speaking colonies in North America and the Caribbean which had been barred to them before 1707. It was no surprise that the only Scottish city to demonstrate any great hostility to Stuart and his Jacobite rebels was Glasgow.

Many of Scotland's political leaders also felt frozen out by the union. The English-dominated government in London ran Scotland under patronage which meant that only men willing to work for England's interests were appointed to positions of power. There were many angry and frustrated politicians in Scotland who felt they were being unjustly denied their place at the pig trough of power. The English also made no secret of the fact that payments had been made to the members of the old Scottish Parliament who voted for the treaty.

Meanwhile, in London, the English establishment could not hide its disgust at the swarms of uncouth Scots who were flooding to the capital in search of fame and fortune. Scots tended to be better educated than Englishmen in those days and were felt to be a threat. Edinburgh and Philadelphia were power houses of progressive thought and both would be occupied by rebel armies in the space of just over 20 years; the Scots rebels ultimately lost, but their North American counterparts succeeded in breaking the English yoke.

But England's desire to control Scotland was neither economic nor intellectual. It was strategic. Even a semi-independent Scotland offered a back door invasion route for any European power at war with England. And the country most likely to be at war with England at the time was France; the two countries were locked in a decades-long struggle for control of the colonies which were being created worldwide thanks to improved sailing ship technology. The French had attempted to disrupt the English war effort by supporting several attempted invasions aimed at restoring James II and later his son James, the 'Old Pretender', to the British throne.

In 1744, the year before Charles landed in Scotland, the famous French Marshal de Saxe had a fleet at anchor waiting for an invasion of England; but the fleet was scattered by a storm and the invasion was cancelled. Charles had been serving a military apprenticeship with the French and had fought at the Battle of Dettingen in Flanders in 1743 against a British army which included his cousin, and later nemesis, King George II's young son, William, Duke of Cumberland.

By the time that Charles, popularly known as Bonnie Prince Charlie, arrived in Scotland with nine followers there was a lot of dissatisfaction in the country with the Treaty of Union. Many people saw the upheaval which his arrival inevitably caused as a chance to renegotiate the deal with England. At first Charles could only attract the support of a few small Highland clans whose principal motivation was a hatred of the most powerful clan in Scotland, the Campbells. The rebellion, if successful, would put the clans who supported Charles firmly in the driving seat, or so it was hoped.

It is the Highlanders and their final charge at Culloden that everyone remembers, but the army that Charles took with him into England had as many Lowlanders as Highlanders in it. Throughout the eight-and-a-half months of the rebellion, the Jacobite Army never exceeded 10,000 men. The Campbells and other clans that stayed loyal to King George II raised 5,000 men to fight for the Hanoverian Army. Other clan chiefs sat firmly on the fence and some even sent their various sons to fight on both sides.

Following his arrival in the Western Highlands, Charles mustered an army of 3,000 clansmen for a march on Edinburgh. He managed to outmanoeuvre the English troops sent into the

Highlands to intercept his army and he reached Edinburgh almost unopposed. The opposing troops, under the command of General John Cope, had to make their way north to Inverness and then on to Aberdeen where ships took them back south to Dunbar on the Firth of Forth to confront the rebels. The best of the British Army was fighting the French in Flanders, which meant that Cope's troops were mainly raw recruits.

The two armies met east of Edinburgh at Prestonpans on 21 September. Cope, a grizzled veteran officer who once served with the Royal Scots, took up a strong position with his flanks protected by a bog on one side and high stone walls built by two local landowners on the other. But a local man guided the rebels safely across the bog overnight and, as the early morning coastal mist cleared, the Highlanders were in position to charge down on the enemy's right flank. Cope barely had time to re-align his troops to face the new threat when the Highland host swept forward. Cope's men fled in terror from the broadsword-swinging and axe-wielding onslaught. For the loss of 40 men, the Jacobites killed 400 of Cope's troops and captured another 1,400.

The only Royal Army in Scotland had been destroyed and the way to England was now open. There were still Royalist garrisons in key fortresses, such as Edinburgh Castle, but the small number of troops they contained meant they posed no threat to the Jacobite's hold on the country. Edinburgh Castle was held by English dragoons who were somehow persuaded to lend money to the Jacobites occupying the city, at a fair rate of interest, before the Scots marched off into England.

The invasion of England was not popular with the rebels. Many of Charles's Scottish advisors wanted to tighten the Jacobite grip on Scotland first and then negotiate from a position of power with the English and their London-Scottish lapdogs. But Charles wasn't concerned with Scotland's interests; his eyes were firmly set on the British throne. Unfortunately, not many English people wanted to see Charles or his father, the 'Old Pretender', on the throne. The Jacobite Army, its ranks swelled by Lowland Scots volunteers following the victory at Prestonpans, marched to within 127 miles of London. But very few Englishmen, with the exception of 200 Episcopalians from Manchester, joined the rebels.

London was reduced to hysteria by the approach of the Jacobites. The Bank of England was besieged by worried depositors demanding their money and it began paying out in six-penny coins to discourage a run on its assets. Anti-Scottish feeling swelled to enormous proportions. The new National Anthem 'God Save The King' called on the Royalist commander-in-chief, Field Marshal George Wade, to crush the 'rebellious Scots'. Not Jacobites or Highlanders – Scots. No mention of Manchester Episcopalians either. The English, at least, knew what the war was really about.

Troops under the command of the Duke of Cumberland were rushed back from Flanders to deal with the Jacobite threat. The Dutch also sent troops to help their British ally and more than half the British Army soldiers under Wade's command were Dutch. The Jacobites, however, managed to evade the two armies sent to block their march to London and reached Derby unmolested.

But enthusiasm for the invasion, never high, was plummeting amongst the Jacobites. Their best general, Lord George Murray, like Cope, a former officer in the Royal Scots, argued strongly for a retreat back to Scotland. Murray believed that without English support and no sign of the promised French invasion, the Jacobites had no chance of capturing London. The way to the capital was also by a third English army and both Wade's and Cumberland's troops were lurking somewhere north of the Jacobite Army. Charles did not trust Murray and he had two spies assigned to monitor him closely and kill him if they saw any sign of treachery. Eventually even Charles admitted that retreat was inevitable and it was finally ordered on 6 December 1745 after a Royalist double agent had exaggerated the number of Royal troops blocking the road to London and thus managed to convince Charles that any further advance would lead to disaster.

The Jacobites slipped past the Royal armies blocking their path again, but Cumberland's troops were soon hard on their heels. The

Jacobites did manage to defeat a Royal army commanded by the brutal Lieutenant-General Henry Hawley (who earned the nickname of 'Hangman' after Culloden) near Falkirk and they continued to retreat north ahead of Cumberland's pursuing troops.

Cumberland was not a great general, but his army presented a major threat; his men were veterans and they were drilled in volley firing, unleashing three deadly waves of lead shot per minute at the enemy. His artillery gunners were better trained than their Jacobite counterparts and their cannon were far superior to the antique ordnance Charles's men had been hauling up and down the country. Though Cumberland's cavalry had a well-deserved reputation for cowardice, he had more mounted men than Charles.

The last thing Charles should have done was challenge Cumberland to a set-piece battle on level ground which gave all the advantages to the redcoated regulars of the British Army, but that is exactly what Charles did, ignoring his generals' advice. Murray and the other Scots commanders favoured a continued retreat into the Western Highlands or at least holding a battle on less favourable ground for the enemy, but Charles chose to fight just east of Inverness on Drummossie Moor. The Scots leaders were goaded into agreeing to fight at Culloden by Charles and his clique of Irish advisors, who accused them of being fair-weather warriors.

The Jacobite Army was half-starved by the time it reached Culloden on 16 April 1746. It had been reinforced by 750 Scots and Irish regular soldiers from the French army but many of the Lowland volunteers had vanished by this stage of the campaign. Charles probably had over 5,000 men at Culloden. His cousin Cumberland had over 8,0000. A bungled night attack on Cumberland's camp at Nairn meant many of Charles's men had had no sleep before the battle.

The Jacobites took up a strong defensive position on Drummossie Moor, protected by the stone walls on both flanks with an area of boggy ground in front of them. The only problem was that Cumberland had no intention of attacking.

Charles placed his Highland clansmen in his front line with the remaining Lowland volunteers, the Irish and Scots regulars of the French Army, and his small cavalry force behind forming the second line and a small third line. Cumberland originally drew his men up in three lines but after surveying the field he then moved two of the three battalions in the third line forward. Five pairs of three-pounder cannon were placed between the regiments holding the front line. Those regiments included the Royal Scots, the King's Own Scottish Borderers and the Royal Scots Fusiliers.

The weather was foul as sleet drove into the gaunt faces of Jacobite troops. There are several examples of men from the same family facing each other across the few hundred yards that separated the two armies. James and John Chisholm stood with the redcoat soldiers of the Royal Scots while their brother Roderick was at the head of the clan's warriors in the Jacobite frontline on the other side of the moor.

Around 1pm the artillery on both sides opened fire. The Royal cannon quickly disabled the Jacobite guns and were soon ripping gaps in the ranks of the Highlanders on the right wing of the Jacobite Army. The Highlanders stood in the face of the cannon fire for what must have seemed like hours, but was probably only 20 minutes. At last, they could stand it no more and the centre and right wings of the Jacobite army charged forward. The bog and the concentrated fire from the Royal regiments in the centre positions sent the Highland charge intended for them swerving to the right. The two English regiments in the path of the now combined centre and right wing of Highlanders took the full brunt of the charge. The funnelling of the Highlanders to the right meant that their ranks were too congested for the traditional close-range volley of musket fire which usually preceded the broadsword charge, but despite this they broke through the two Royal regiments.

The second line of Royal troops then unleashed a ruthless volley which cut down both the advancing Highlanders and many of the redcoats still battling in the front line. Many of the Highlanders realised at this point that there was little chance of breaking through the second line of Royal troops and began to drift back from the fighting. That drift became a rush when it was realised that the Campbell troops with the Royal Army had broken down the walls protecting the Highlanders' right flank and English dragoons were now swarming onto the battlefield behind the fighting.

Meanwhile, the Macdonald clansmen who made up the front line of the Jacobite left wing were making little progress in the face of the Royal Army's cannon and disciplined volleys of musket fire. The bog which had sent the Highlanders in the centre swerving to the right was now hampering the Macdonalds' advance as well. The Highland retreat soon became widespread and it was left to the Irish and Scots regulars from the French army to cover the withdrawal of what was left of the Jacobite Army back towards Inverness.

Charles had quit the battlefield long before then. Some sources say he had to be dragged away, others that he could not leave quickly enough. He died in Rome 42 years after the battle, a moody, violent, drunken wreck.

The English dragoons chased the fleeing Jacobites all the way to Inverness and cut down every man, woman and child they came across on the way. Meanwhile, the Royal Army was advancing across the battlefield systematically shooting and bayoneting the Jacobite wounded where they lay. Cumberland justified the slaughter by claiming the Jacobites had been ordered to 'give no quarter', which was a lie. Another lie was told when 12 wounded Jacobites were persuaded to come out of a farmhouse they were sheltering in with a promise of medical attention. They were murdered on the spot. A nearby barn containing 30 wounded Jacobites was burned to the ground with them still inside. An estimated 1,250 Jacobites were killed in the battle or murdered by Cumberland's troops afterwards. The redcoats lost around 360 men dead and wounded, nearly all from the two English regiments which took the brunt of the Highland charge.

More than half of the Jacobite Army was still intact after the battle but the survivors turned for home when it became apparent that Charles was now on the run and had no interest in continuing the rebellion. He would be picked up by a French ship months later.

Cumberland's troops then fanned out across the Highlands to

subjugate the clans. They were not too fussy about whose side people had been on during the rebellion; men were killed, women were raped, cattle were driven off and homes were burned. Before houses were put to the torch, the soldiers usually helped themselves to any loot they could find. Three Scottish officers, Major I Lockhart, Captain Caroline Scott and Captain John Fergussone, took a particular delight in leading the raiding parties and instilling terror in the glens.

Laws were then introduced which proscribed Highlanders from wearing kilts, playing bagpipes or carrying arms. It was the beginning of the end of the clan system in Scotland. While there can be little doubt that economic realities would have eventually changed the centuries-old way of life most Highlanders led, the brutal and indiscriminate destruction unleashed after Culloden made the change far more catastrophic than it might have been.

Englishman Dr Samuel Johnson, no great admirer of the Scots as a race, commented on Culloden, the last major land battle on British soil, by echoing a version of the quote the Roman historian Tacitus had given on Scotland's first recorded battle almost 1,700 years before: 'they make a desolation and call it peace'.

Thousands of Scots were thrown into prison where many died in appalling conditions; the lucky ones were sold into slavery in North America and the Caribbean. Once again, the terms of the Treaty of Union were ignored as the treaty stated that Scots in Scotland would be dealt with under Scots law. But nearly all the prisoners were shipped to England for what passed as their trials. Sixteen years after Culloden, two Scottish officers attending a play in London after fighting with the British Army in Cuba were hissed at by the rest of the audience and had fruit thrown at them to chants of, 'No Scots! No Scots!'

A few years later, the expansion of the British Empire meant jobs for all, English or Scot and Scottish manufacturing boomed in response. As Britain's Empire grew so did the role of the Scots in managing it and many families of clansmen who were involved in Culloden were to benefit from it.

DEATH PROPHESIED

TICONDEROGA 1758

Major Duncan Campbell knew his day to die had come. Few of the other members of the Black Watch who died alongside him in the wooded North American wilderness in July 1758 shared his sense of certain doom. But then, none of them had been visited by a ghost the night before the battle. Although Campbell's fellow officers knew that the ghost had appeared in the past to predict that the Argyllshire man would die at Ticonderoga, their orders were for an attack on Fort Carillon. When it was realised that Fort Carillon was known to the Indians as Ticonderoga, the officers kept the information from him. The ghost that re-appeared to Campbell the night before the attack on the fort had revealed the secret his fellow officers had been keeping from him.

The ghost story began three years previously when Campbell encountered a distraught and frightened man on Ben Cruachan, near his home at Inverawe, Argyll. The man begged for shelter from the avenging relatives of a man he claimed to have killed by accident and Campbell agreed to hide him. Campbell later regretted giving his word of honour to the fugitive when he learned that the victim has been one of his close cousins.

For three days he sheltered the killer until the man managed to escape from the neighbourhood safely. The ghost of his murdered relative appeared to Campbell on two successive nights while he was sheltering the killer and begged to be avenged. When Campbell refused, the ghost predicted that they would meet again – at Ticonderoga.

Campbell was one of several members of his clan amongst the officers of the Black Watch. It had been raised in 1725 as a paramilitary police force at a time when the Highlands were lawless and many clans were still loyal to the deposed Stewart royal family. In 1739 the Black Watch was converted into a regular British army regiment and six years later proved its worth at the defeat of the British army at the Battle of Fontenoy in Flanders under the command of the Duke of Cumberland.

After he had crushed the Highland clans in the aftermath of the Battle of Culloden in 1746, it was decided the warlike spirit of the Highland clans could be better harnessed to serve the cause of the growing British Empire. Highlanders had defeated two British armies before Cumberland's victory at Culloden and it was hoped that their devastating broadsword-swinging charge would prove equally effective ten years later when war erupted with France again.

Many Highlanders, with their long tribal warrior tradition, did not care who they fought against, as long as they fought someone. They flocked to join the new regiments being raised for the war against the French; the prospect of regular rations, adventure and a good fight was too great to resist. When the Black Watch sailed for New York in 1756 it still contained 200 veterans from the Battle of Fontenoy in the ranks and they were now joined by men from the clans once loyal to the Jacobite cause.

As the Black Watch joined the biggest British army ever assembled in North America to that date, the British Government finally hoped to conquer Canada and wrest the country from the French.

Two armies were to be sent north to invade Canada. The Black Watch were part of a force that was to seize Fort Carillon at the strategically important junction of Lake George and Lake Champlain; this would open the route to the French-held city of Montreal. The second force was to attack down the Gulf of St

Lawrence under General James Wolfe and capture the capital of New France, as Canada was also known at the time, at Quebec.

The force which included the Black Watch was originally commanded by Lord Loudon, but he was recalled to London for political reasons and his second-in-command General James Abercrombie took over. Good-natured but prone to gout, the 52-year-old Banffshire man had not enjoyed a particularly distinguished military career. He spent almost 20 years as a captain and though regarded as a good second-in-command, there were serious doubts about him as a battlefield commander.

Fortunately, he had as second-in-command 34-year-old Lord Howe, a grandson of George I, who was regarded by many as the finest officer in the British Army. He ordered his men to adapt their uniforms to frontier warfare by cutting short their long coats and even encouraged them to carry tomahawks. Tragically, Howe was shot dead through the heart in a skirmish with French troops before the main battle.

Approximately 16,000 British and American colonial troops outnumbered the French by four-to-one and Fort Carillon was badly positioned on a promontory overlooked by a ridge where cannon could be set up to bombard it. Worse for the French, the fort only had room for around 1,000 troops. However, what the French did have was a highly competent soldier in command, the Marquis Louis-Joseph de Montcalm.

When the French saw a seven-mile long convoy of more than 1,000 boats filled with troops and supplies coming down Lake George, they retreated from their defensive positions along the shoreline near the fort. Instead, Montcalm decided to fortify the dominant ridge about a mile from the fort against the British. His men hacked and dug for more than 24 hours to build a 10ft-high stockade along the ridge with loopholes cut in the logs for muskets to fire through and swivel guns, effectively oversized shotguns, positioned on top. The best marksmen amongst the French were detailed to man the loopholes while their comrades reloaded their muskets as quickly as possible and passed them back. This gave the

French a rate of fire of six-rounds a minute, twice the usual battlefield rate.

But the biggest problem the British faced was getting through the tangle of felled trees the French had positioned in front of the stockade. The branches were positioned to create a mass of sharpened points sticking out from the trees to create an obstacle similar to a modern barbed-wire entanglement. The British badly underestimated the strength of this and other French defences. A reconnaissance party had wrongly identified a lightly held advance post as the main stockade and reported it could have been knocked over with a shoulder charge. Abercrombie's failure to have the French defences properly scouted was all the more surprising when the fact that his force included the famed Rogers' Rangers, clad in green and filled with expert American woodsmen, and 400 Iroquois Indians was taken into account.

Believing Montcalm was about to be reinforced by a further 3,000 Frenchmen at any moment, Abercrombie decided not to wait for his heavy artillery before launching his main attack on the stockade. Some artillery guns were landed from rafts on a stretch of shore across a small inlet from Fort Carillon to blast the French positions from the flank. Poor reconnaissance of the landing point and some well-aimed fire from the French cannon turned the landing area into a disaster.

The uninspired and uninspiring Abercrombie came up with a plan that involved drawing his 10,000 British regulars up into three columns and marching them simultaneously at the stockade. The attack was scheduled for the morning of 8 July, two days after the initial landings from Lake George; Abercrombie stationed himself in a command post two miles behind the fighting.

It took the British until almost lunchtime to reach a point within musket range of the French stockade and things started to go wrong pretty quickly. One of the American colonial regiments which was supposed to be protecting the flank of the British regulars came under fire from a previously unsuspected French position and for some reason the men of Rogers' Rangers disappeared in entirely the wrong direction. Then one of the British column commanders refused to delay his assault in order to let the other two columns get into their attack positions and launched his men at the stockade unsupported. The men quickly became entangled in the forest of sharpened branches in front of the stockade.

The Black Watch were supposed to be held in reserve, but Major Campbell and his officers were unable to restrain their soldiers and they launched their own unauthorised charge at the French stockade using their broadswords to hack through the maze of fallen trees and branches in their path. An officer of another regiment described the Highlanders as charging like 'roaring lions breaking their chains'.

Twice the officers managed to reform the Highlanders and launch them at the stockade. The wounded shouted encouragement to their frenzied colleagues as they slashed at the tree branches preventing them from reaching the stockade. The furious and frustrated Highlanders appeared more intent on revenging their dead than concerned for their own lives.

The third attack came closest to success and appears to have been inspired by a misunderstanding. In the late 1750s the signal for a temporary truce during a battle was a red flag and some of the British thought they saw one being waved from the stockade. There was some confusion about who was surrendering to whom and a group of British troops who then advanced to take prisoners was blasted by a sudden French volley of musket fire.

The Black Watch men were enraged by this apparent treachery and doubled their efforts to clear a way to the stockade by scrambling up onto each other's shoulders to surmount it. Some of the Highlanders even began hacking steps out of the logs of the stockade but most were bayoneted and killed as they reached the top.

However, Captain John Campbell, a man of six foot and wielding a broadsword, managed to lead 20 of his men over the top. Spotting the breakthrough, Montcalm himself, clad in shirtsleeves, led a furious counter attack which left only seven of Campbell's men alive to surrender. The Highlanders continued to scramble at the stockade despite being blasted again and again by the French muskets. It was only when they ran out of ammunition that they finally obeyed Abercrombie's repeated orders to retreat. The French held their fire when they saw the Highlanders pulling back and even let them carry off their wounded. Out of an original strength of around 1,000 men, the Black Watch lost 314 men and suffered 333 wounded. The total number of dead for the whole British force was only 464.

By 5pm most of the British were in retreat, though some elected to stay under the cover of the fallen trees until dark when they could sneak away without getting a French musket ball in the back. Montcalm decided not risk sending his still outnumbered troops in pursuit of the retreating British. Surprisingly, his casualty rate was higher than the British one. Although he lost 350 dead and wounded against the British total of 1,500, the French casualty rate was 13% compared to the British rate of 11%. However, it was beyond all doubt a French victory.

Montcalm died a year later defending Quebec City in a battle which also claimed the life of his opponent General James Wolfe. The Black Watch chose not to regard the attack on Fort Carillon as a disaster but instead as a testimony to the fighting spirit of Highland troops, but it was more than a year before the battalion was deemed fit to fight again. The survivors of Ticonderoga returned in 1759 with a new British army and this time the French gave up the fort without a fight and escaped down Lake Champlain.

HEADLESS HORROR

FORT DU QUÈSNE 1758

The men of the Montgomerie Highlanders could not contain their rage when they came across the severed and decaying heads of their comrades displayed on stakes alongside a trail through the North American wilderness in November 1758. They had been decapitated a few weeks earlier by Indians following a disastrous attack on the French-held Fort Du Quèsne at the strategically important junction of the Monongahela and Allegheny rivers.

Each stake was draped with a blood-stained kilt as a sign of the contempt the Indians had for the Scots they called 'petticoat warriors'. The American militia troops leading the British march to Fort Du Quèsne passed the grim display in silence, but the Highlanders who followed them began shouting in outrage when they saw it. Suddenly the militia were pushed aside by a rush of broadsword brandishing Highlanders intent on killing any Frenchman or Indian they could find in the fort. But the fort, on the site of present-day Pittsburgh, had been abandoned and burned the night before. All the Highlanders found were some smouldering timbers.

The Highlanders had been brought to North America as part of a British army sent to fight the French and hopefully drive them out of Canada once and for all. The conflict was the latest in a series of wars between France and Britain which had been going on for more than 60 years in continental Europe; the fighting spread across the world as both countries gained overseas colonies. The latest war appeared to offer the British an excellent chance to grab the French colonies in Canada, India and the Caribbean.

The raising of the Montgomerie Highlanders in 1757 was a risk for the British Government because only 11 years before several of the clans from which it was drawn had sent men to fight against it at Culloden. The new regiment relied heavily on former rebel clans such as the MacDonalds, MacLeans, MacPhersons and Camerons for recruits to fight against the French. Even then, the regiment was forced to take on 59 Lowland Scots to reach its full strength of just over 1,400 men. The British Army was scoured for Gaelic-speakers who were drafted into the new regiment to provide it with a core of experienced sergeants and corporals.

Shortly after arriving in South Carolina, the new regiment was sent north to join an expedition to capture Fort Du Quèsne under the command of the failed-medical-student-turned-soldier from Fife, Brigadier-General John Forbes. Forbes, a former commander of the Royal Scots Greys, favoured a slow march to the fort which would give the Indians allied to the French plenty of time to desert. The French depended heavily on the warriors of the Shawnee, Huron, Miami, Ottawa and Pottawattamie tribes to support their war effort. As Forbes and his men marched towards Fort Du Quèsne, British agents were working hard to persuade the Indians to change sides, or at least declare themselves neutral.

The British advance involved hacking a road through the virgin forest, but cutting down trees and digging roads were not attractive pursuits for the men of the Montgomerie Highlanders and their leader Major James Grant. When the 6,000-strong British army reached a point 50 miles from Fort Du Quèsne, Grant begged to be allowed to take 400 of his men on ahead to conduct a reconnaissance mission. Forbes was ill, but his Swiss-born deputy Colonel Henry Bouquet gave permission for the raid and added 450 American militiamen to Grant's force. Most of the troops under Forbes's command were American militiamen, including future president George Washington, or regular troops recruited in

America as members of the Royal American Regiment. Grant and his men spent five days making their way through the woods and came within sight of Fort Du Quèsne on 14 September. It is a tribute to Grant's military skill that during the march he managed to avoid the Indian scouts the French had placed in the forest and reach a point within half-a-mile of the fort without his force being detected. Forbes split his men into several groups and placed the American militiamen in ambush positions on the forest trail that led to the fort. It would appear his plan was to approach the fort with his Highlanders in the hope of luring the French and their Indian allies into a trap. To make it easier for his men to recognise each other in the early morning gloom, he ordered them to pull their spare white shirts over their red uniform jackets.

It seems that Grant greatly underestimated the number of men at the fort; He believed there were no more than 200 inside but the number was closer to 800. His first attempt to draw the garrison out by sending a small party of men to burn down some outbuildings failed. Then he sent 100 Highlanders marching boldly towards the fort but this also failed to bring a response; the fort remained silent and Grant must have been wondering if it had already been abandoned. He then ordered his piper to strike up a tune with the drummers accompanying the force beating out a wake-up call but this backfired as all hell broke loose with the 800 French troops and Indian warriors in the fort charging out to engage the Scots. Grant suddenly realised he was badly outnumbered but the enemy where thrown into disorder when Highlanders began firing disciplined volleys of musket fire into them. What Grant had not realised was that there was a large Indian war party camped downriver from the Fort and when they heard the shooting, they came running. The British were surprised from behind and soon the men he had hidden in ambush positions along the trail were running for their lives from the Indians.

The men from the fort then rallied and began to close in on Forbes's men from all sides. His militiamen took cover in the trees but the Highlanders remained standing in the open in tightly packed ranks, blasting volley after volley at the French and Indians who were darting between the trees around them. The Highland ranks soon began to thin out as hidden French and Indian marksmen picked the Scots off. Eventually, the Highlanders could no longer stand being sniped at and started to run.

Grant and about a dozen men fought their way through the bush and forest to where about 50 militiamen were guarding the baggage train. He hoped to make a final stand there against the howling Indians who were chasing him, but after a brief exchange of fire, the militiamen took to their heels. Grant later complained in a letter to Forbes that, 'orders were of no purpose. Fear had got the better of every other passion and I hope I shall never see again such panic amongst the troops'.

General Forbes, writing after the tragedy at Fort Du Quèsne, said he could only conclude that Grant had temporarily lost his wits. Washington described Grant's actions as '... [a] very ill-concerted, or very ill-executed plan, perhaps both; but it seems to be generally acknowledged, that Major Grant exceeded his orders and that no disposition was made for engaging.' Despite the disaster at Fort Du Quèsne, Grant was later given command of an expedition to crush the Cherokee Indians of South Carolina.

Grant was quickly made prisoner and sent by the French to Quebec City as a possible bargaining chip in negotiations with the British. Many of the men who were taken prisoner at Fort Du Quèsne were not so lucky. No-one will ever know how many of them died in battle and how many were sadistically tortured to death afterwards. Indians armed with clubs stood on either side of the trail which led to the fort and forced their prisoners to run the gauntlet between them. Many of the Scots failed to survive the beating their received on the run. The severed heads and kilts of the murdered Highlanders were then placed on sharpened stakes lining a three-mile stretch of the trail; the same stretch that had so enraged the rest of the regiment when they approached the fort on 25 November.

One Highlander took particular note of the barbaric fate of his comrades at the hands of the Indians. When Allan Macpherson was captured after the regiment was sent south with Grant to fight the Cherokee, he began boasting to his captors that he was invincible. He claimed to know of a magic ointment that would protect him from the harm they could do him. Of course, the Indians demanded a demonstration and Macpherson was taken off into the forest to gather the herbs needed to make the ointment. After rubbing some of the concoction he had brewed up onto his neck, Macpherson invited one of the Cherokees to attempt to sever his head with a war axe. The warrior swung … and off came Macpherson's head. The Indians were so impressed by the ingenious trick the Highlander had used to escape torture that they spared the lives of their other prisoners.

After Grant's defeat at Fort Du Quèsne, the Indians started to drift away from the French base. Winter was coming and they had work to do back home if their families were to survive until spring. Without their Indian allies, and cut off from their supply lines and reinforcements by successful British attacks on French forts elsewhere, the garrison was forced to abandon Fort Du Quèsne. The night before Forbes and his men were expected to reach the fort, the French set it alight and escaped in boats.

The force which marched into the fort included about 100 of the Highlanders who had managed to escape through the forest after Grant's defeat; of approximately 400 Highlanders who marched to the fort with Grant, 104 were killed and 219 were wounded. Many of the survivors opted to make their home in North America when the regiment was disbanded in 1763 following the defeat of the French and the conquest of Canada, but most would never forget or forgive the terrible scene that greeted them on that final march to Fort Du Quèsne in November 1758.

NO TEA PARTY

BOSTON HARBOUR 1776

The last thing that the 200 or so Highland soldiers sent to fight the rebels during the American Revolution expected was that their part in the war would be over before they even set foot on shore. The poor communications across the Atlantic Ocean at the time which dogged the British throughout the war, proved fatal for eight of the Scots when their troopship sailed into Boston Harbour, unaware that it was now in rebel hands. Scots, particularly Highland Scots, had flocked to fight in the war against the 13 most southerly of the British colonies in North America when they rebelled in 1776.

Amongst the units sent to fight the rebels was the 71st Highland Regiment, popularly known as the Fraser Highlanders. The regiment had first fought in North America almost 20 years before against the French; it was part of the British army that had captured Quebec in 1759 and laid the final foundations for the conquest of French-held Canada. At the end of the war against the French it was decided to disband the regiment; but when the colonies revolted, the regiment was resurrected.

Major-General Simon Fraser of Lovat contracted with the British Government to raise two battalions of troops for service in North America. In April 1776 he had 2,340 men mustered at Stirling, then the gateway between the Gaelic-speaking Highlands and the English-speaking Lowlands. The men were marched to Glasgow, a city which had grown rich trading across the Atlantic with the North American colonies. There they were joined by troops from the 42nd Royal Highland Regiment, better known as the Black Watch. Altogether around 3,000 Highland soldiers were gathered in Glasgow for transportation across the Atlantic. Not surprisingly, in a city with such close connections to the colonies, news of the 'Scotch Fleet' reached North America long before the 30 ships carrying the soldiers did.

In June 1776 the vessels were approaching the American coast when a storm scattered the fleet. While some transports limped into New York and Halifax over the next few weeks, others made for Boston but what their captains did not know was that Boston was no longer in British hands. The British army had pulled out two months earlier and no ships had been stationed off the port to warn incoming shipping that the rebels now controlled Boston.

The rebels could not believe their luck when two troop ships laden with more than 200 members of the 71st Highlanders sailed into Boston Harbour without a Royal Navy escort. A swarm of privateers, merchant ships armed with cannon and issued with licences to capture enemy shipping, effectively legal pirates, sailed out to greet them.

The *George* and the *Annabella* were outgunned but put up a good fight; they might even have escaped if they had not become becalmed in the harbour, giving the rebels time to move their shore-based cannons into a better position to blast the enemy. The sailors on the *George*, with the exception of their captain, had wanted to surrender earlier, but Lieutenant-Colonel Archibald Campbell of the 71st Highlanders refused to quit the fight. But as the cannon balls continued to smash into the *George*, even Campbell finally accepted that the situation was hopeless. By the time he agreed to surrender, eight of his men, including his second-in-command Major Robert Menzies, had been killed. Campbell later wrote about his decision to surrender.

'On our refusing to strike the British flag, the action was renewed, with a good deal of warmth on both sides; and it was our misfortune, after a sharp combat of an hour and a half, to have expended every shot that we had for our artillery.

'Under such circumstances, hemmed in, as we were, with six privateers, in the middle of the enemy's harbour, beset with dead calm, without the power of escaping, or even the most distant hope of relief, I thought it my duty not to sacrifice the lives of gallant men wantonly in the arduous attempt of an evident impossibility.'

Campbell and 198 of his men were quickly brought ashore and marched off into captivity. As they marched, they were jeered and cursed at by the people of Boston and the surrounding area who were all too aware of the number of Scots joining the British Army to fight against the rebels.

'On our journey no slaves were ever served as we were,' wrote one of the Highlanders later. 'Through every village, town and hamlet that we passed, the women and children, and indeed some of the men amongst them, came out and loaded us with the most rascally epithets, calling us "Rascally cut-throat dogs, Murderers, Blood-hounds", but what vexed me most was their continually slandering our country, on which they threw the most infamous invectives: to this they added showers of dirt and filth, and now and then a stone.'

It has been estimated that more than 20,000 Scots, and perhaps as many as 65,000, volunteered to help King George III put down the colonial rebellion at a time when the war was unpopular in England and recruits were hard to find.

Campbell was thrown in a dungeon in retaliation for the alleged mistreatment of rebel prisoners by the British. It turned out that the allegations against the British were untrue, but it took the personal intervention of General George Washington before Campbell received decent treatment; he was finally exchanged for Vermont rebel leader Ethan Allen after two years as a prisoner. Before the Revolution, Allen had become infamous for terrorizing settlers caught up in a boundary dispute between the Vermont and New York colonies. Several of the settlers involved in Allen's war of terror were former members of Highland regiments who had taken their discharge after the fall of Quebec and settled in the area. For this Allen terrorised them because their land titles had been issued in New York and not Vermont; the authorities in New York had put a price of £300 on Allen's head.

The members of the 71st Highlanders whose transport ships had reached the safety of the British-held ports after the storm soon found soon themselves involved in fighting near New York City. The rebels were commanded by George Washington, an old friend of the 71st Highlanders' commander Lieutenant-Colonel John Maitland with whom he had served in the war against the French. Maitland wrote to Washington that he had ordered his men to wear red hackles (more commonly associated with the Black Watch) in their bonnets so that his old friend could see what a fine job they were doing against him.

It is no longer clear how many ships of the British fleet were captured by the rebels. The records are contradictory and some suggest as many as seven transports and 500 men fell into enemy hands. One company from the Black Watch, numbering about 100 men, was captured twice. After the storm, their ship, the *Oxford*, was captured by a privateer but they managed to overpower their captors and took the ship to Jamestown in Virginia. Alas, like Boston, Jamestown was by that time in rebel hands and they became prisoners of war for second time.

After his release in 1778, Campbell led two battalions of the 71st Highlanders on an expedition which captured Georgia for the British.

KING GEORGE AND
THE BROADSWORDS!

MOORE'S CREEK 1776

Highland heroine Flora MacDonald taking the side of King George III in the American Revolution? Surely not? The woman who smuggled Bonnie Prince Charlie to safety after his rebel Highland army was defeated at Culloden in 1746 managed to choose the wrong side again 30 years later when she lived in North Carolina. But perhaps her decision to back George III should not be such a surprise after all. Her husband Allen, like many of the Highland gentry at the time, had served in the British Army during the Jacobite rebellion. MacDonald's stepfather, Hugh MacDonald, known to his tenants as One-eyed Hugh, was also a British officer and some believe it was One-eyed Hugh who masterminded the escape of the Bonnie Prince from Uist to Skye disguised at his step-daughter's servant Betty Burke. That escapade earned Flora MacDonald a year in the Tower of London and fame as the saviour of the charming but flawed Charles Edward Stuart.

When Allen and Flora MacDonald sailed from Campbeltown in Scotland to Campbeltown, North Carolina, in 1774, they were joining a Highland exodus to the Cape Fear area which had begun in the early 1730s. The couple already had several relations, including One-eyed Hugh, living there. Curiously, they first settled in Cumberland County, hardly a placename expected to find favour with die-hard Jacobites in view of the devastation of the Highlands ordered by the Duke of Cumberland after Culloden.

The couple had arrived in North America at a turbulent time. The conquest of Canada and the exodus of the French had elimi- nated a major thorn in the side of the English-speaking colonists further south. When the British Government in London tried to recoup part of the cost of the war against the French from the colonists, the move was met with outrage. With the French threat removed, the colonists saw little need at all to pay for a British army in North America. Many in the 13 colonies demanded represen- tation in the British parliament if they were going to be taxed by it. The slogan went up: No taxation without representation!

Others had more ambitious aims; they wanted the British out altogether. The only major barriers now for access to the massive land and mineral wealth of North America were the Indian tribes. The British Government had been too willing, in the colonists' eyes, to sign treaties with the Indians instead of wiping them out. Some of the colonial elite, including future US President George Washington, had even been selling land already assigned by treaty to the Indians.

In North Carolina and many of the other southern states there was little intellectual demand for more representative democracy and the curbing of King George III's powers. In the South the revolution was seen as a chance for a power-grab by the handful of families that had become rich through the use of slaves to harvest the rice crop. With the British gone, the Rice Kings would be undis- puted masters of the southern states. The Highlanders had little to gain by supporting the Rice Kings but many were reluctant to back a British Government which had sent its redcoated soldiers to pillage and burn their way across much of the Highlands 30 years before in the wake of the rebel defeat at Culloden.

The truth about the American Revolution was that it was really America's first civil war. About one-third of the population was for the revolution, one-third was against and one-third just wanted to be left alone. But the revolutionaries worked on the principle that 'if you're not for us, you're against us,' and targeted the uncommitted one-third with a campaign of terror and intimi- dation. It was hard to stay uncommitted for long.

A series of appalling military and political blunders made the British side a less attractive bet as time went on and by the end of the war most of those who started out uncommitted were siding with the revolutionaries. In the early stages of the revolution, the Highlanders were courted by both sides as Highland troops serving in the British Army during the war against France had gained an excellent reputation as light infantry. The leaders of the Highland community in Cape Fear, including the MacDonalds, were wooed by both the rebel-controlled North Carolina Provincial Council and the ousted British Governor, Josiah Martin. In the end, Martin persuaded the Highlanders to help him regain control of North Carolina and throw their lot in on King George III's side.

In the run-up to the war the British had decided to recruit a regiment from the Highlanders who had settled in North America. These included soldiers from the Highland regiments that had fought against the French and accepted land grants when the war ended. The regiment was to be known as the Royal Highland Emigrants and would have two battalions of about 1,000 men each. One battalion was to be recruited in what are now the Canadian provinces of Ontario and Quebec and in New York State. The men from the other battalion would come from Nova Scotia and North Carolina. Recruits were offered 200 acres of land and 20 years' exemption from taxes.

The MacDonalds became central to the recruitment drive in North Carolina. Both Flora MacDonald's husband and her stepfather took leading roles in persuading their fellow Highlanders to join up. Flora's son-in-law Alexander MacLeod was also a former army officer. Governor Martin swore in the recruits for the Royal Highland Emigrants as colonial militia until they could join the rest of the British Army.

The 1,600 Highlanders were to march to the coast to join Major-General Henry Clinton who was planning to land with a force to seize Charleston, the richest port in North America guarded only by a half-built fort manned by poorly trained rebels. The plan called for the Highlanders to meet up with Clinton on the coast south of Wilmington to prepare for the capture of Charleston.

The rebels sent troops to block the Highlanders' march. Only about half the Highlanders were armed and they were keen to avoid a clash with the rebels before they joined forces with Clinton. The closer the Highlanders got to the coast, the fewer route options they had. The Highlanders' march became a game of hide-and-seek with the rebels until they approached the narrow wooden bridge over Moore's Creek about 20 miles from Wilmington. The rebels realised that it was a pretty safe bet that the Scots would try to use the bridge which spanned the meandering 35-ft-wide creek and they raced to get there first. A small force of rebels reached the bridge two days before the Highlanders on 25 February and was reinforced next day by a larger group.

The rebel commander, Colonel Richard Caswell, then positioned about 850 men near the western approach to the bridge and a smaller force of around 150 camped on the far side of the creek under the command of Colonel Alexander Lillington. They had a two-and-a-half-pounder cannon, christened *Old Mother Covington*, and a half-pounder swivel gun, which was basically a giant shotgun.

The Highlanders had been joined by this time by around 130 fellow loyalists and the joint force was commanded by Major Donald MacDonald, a Gaelic-speaking army officer sent by the British to train and organise his fellow Scots. However, MacDonald took sick around the time that the loyalists reached the Moore's Creek area and command was given to his assistant, another Gaelic speaker, Captain Donald MacLeod.

The loyalists made camp about six miles from the rebel positions at the bridge on the night of 26 February 1776. It was decided to send a certain Alexander MacLean and 75 hand-picked swordsmen ahead to seize the bridge if they could; they arrived to find Caswell and his men had retreated across the creek.

What they did not realise was that the rebels had partially demolished the bridge by pulling up several planks and greased what was still left standing to make crossing a slow and hazardous process. The rebels were also building an earth fort on the far side of the bridge. MacLean and his men were then challenged as they approached the bridge by rebel sentries who called out 'Friend or Foe?' MacLean replied 'Friend … of the king' before retreating into the darkness.

A council-of-war at the loyalist camp ruled out bypassing the bridge and attempting to reach Wilmington by another route. Instead, the Highlanders decided on an old-fashioned broadsword charge to storm across the bridge. Twice during the 1745 Jacobite rebellion the Highlanders had routed British government troops with a charge, so they believed it would work just as well, if not better, against a rebel rabble. As dawn was breaking on the morning of 27 February, the Highlanders charged the bridge with pipes blaring and drums beating. Their war cry was 'King George and broadswords!'.

When the Highlanders reached the bridge, several plunged into the water through the gaps left where the rebels had pulled up the planks; the rest blundered on towards the rebels who were standing silently behind their earthen rampart with muskets primed and *Old Mother Covington* waiting to fire. It was almost all over in an instant. The first volley of musket fire combined with the blast of shot from *Old Mother Covington* carried away the Highlanders' front line. MacLeod and MacLean were amongst those killed instantly.

The Highlanders broke and ran, clambering over each other to get back across the bridge. But the rebels had no intention of letting them escape to fight another day. They rounded up 850 loyalists and a tidy pile of weapons, including 150 broadswords.

Allen MacDonald, who later claimed to have assumed command, was captured with two of his sons. The younger one, James, was returned to his mother, but Allen and his son Alexander were marched off into captivity with the other surviving officers.

Eventually, Allen and Alexander were exchanged for rebel prisoners held by the British. Allen then joined the British Army at New York where he commanded a force of around 100 North Carolinians before being stationed for the rest of the war in Halifax,

Nova Scotia, with the Royal Highland Emigrants. After the war ended, he took a land grant of 3,000 acres on the banks of the Kennetcook River in Nova Scotia as a reward for his services to King George III. But a lack of the funds needed to develop the land meant he had to give the farm up after a year and return to Scotland.

His wife had already gone back. The rebels in North Carolina had made life uncomfortable for her after Moore's Creek and after about a year she headed north to British-held New York. In 1779 she sailed back to Scotland and the Isle of Skye where she died 11 years later.

Clinton's attempt to capture Charleston collapsed when the attack on the half-built fort on Sullivan's Island at the mouth of the city's harbour was badly bungled. North Carolina was soon firmly in rebel hands and the state was the first to vote for complete independence from Britain.

The Highland defeat had consequences well beyond the size of the forces involved. If they had reached Wilmington, then Clinton might have captured Charleston and the British might have regained control of the southern states. After that, the war might have been won before the French came over to the side of rebels and tipped the balance of power in their favour.

ROCKETMEN

POLLILUR 1780

Rocket technology is nothing new, but how many people know of the decisive part it played in a battle in India in 1780 which cost around 200 Scottish soldiers their lives? The men of the 73rd Highlanders were part of a column which had been holding its own against swarms of enemy cavalry near the village of Pollilur in southeastern India until a rocket blew its ammunition wagons to smithereens.

The Highlanders were members of the elite grenadier and light companies of the regiment which had been sent to help rescue the column which was in danger of being overwhelmed by Indian troops sent to prevent it reaching the main British army camped nearby.

In those days Highland regiments were filled with real Highlanders. When Lord MacLeod raised the 73rd Highlanders in 1777 the regiment contained 840 men from the Highland Counties, 236 Lowlanders and 34 English or Irishmen. MacLeod and his men were sent to India where they joined an army commanded by Major-General Hector Munro which was trying to repel an invasion of the pro-British Indian state of Carnatic by troops from pro-French Mysore. Although the ruler of Carnatic was pro-British, many of his subjects looked upon the Mysoreans and their ruler Hyder Ali as liberators.

Ali, a Shia Muslim adventurer who ruled a mainly Hindu state, had built up a formidable army of almost 100,000 men for the invasion. Almost half his troops were cavalry but the army also included 20,000 regular soldiers commanded by European officers and 100 cannon. The Indians were also masters of rocket technology. Rockets had been in use by the Chinese for hundreds of years but the Indians had refined them into weapons that could shoot an explosive warhead into the ranks of the enemy at ranges up to 1,000 yards. In skilled hands, the rockets could be surprisingly accurate. The British had encountered them in battles against Indian troops as far back as 1755 but they had never played the same decisive role that they were to at Pollilur.

To make the best use of his massive superiority in cavalry, Hyder Ali wanted to fight a war of rapid movement which would allow his troops to cut off and destroy isolated columns of British troops before they could be assembled into one army. His first priority was to prevent a column of 3,000 men under Colonel Baillie joining forces with the main British army of 6,000 men under the command of Munro. Lord MacLeod had wanted Baillie to come to British-held port of Madras but Munro insisted on marching his men from the city to Conjeveram, 40 miles inland, to meet him.

Munro reached Conjeveram unmolested and waited for Baillie and his men to arrive. Reports soon came in that Baillie had reached a distance of 15 miles from the meeting point when he encountered serious opposition from the Mysoreans. Baillie had beaten off an attack by a force of 8,000 men under the command of Ali's son, Tipu Sultan but now wanted Munro to come to him, rather than the other way around.

Instead, Munro sent 800 reinforcements to Baillie and told him to continue his march to Conjeveram. The reinforcements comprised 200 men from the 73rd Highlanders, 200 troops from the East India Company's Madras European Regiment and 400 locally recruited Indian sepoys in the pay of the company. Britain's holdings in India at the time were run by the East India Company, a private concern with close ties to the government, which had its own private army of sepoys and white mercenaries.

The reinforcements sent by Munro were commanded by a Colonel Fletcher who suspected that the Indian guides assigned to him where planning to lead the troops into a Mysorean ambush. During the march, Fletcher suddenly ordered an unanticipated change of direction and successfully evaded the ambush set for his small column.

After Fletcher's men arrived, Baillie resumed the march from his camp at Perambaukum towards Conjeveram and the main British army. But when the Mysoreans had realised Munro had no plans to leave Conjeveram they saw their chance to destroy Baillie's column without interference from the main British army. Hyder Ali joined his son with 18,000 more cavalry, 30,000 infantry and 60 cannon to ambush Baillie's men near the village of Pollilur. The cannon were hidden in positions where they could fire into the village from three sides once Baillie's men reached it. But the cannon opened fire too soon and Baillie was able to pull his men back from the trap. Baillie's own artillery force of 10 cannons was soon in action against the Mysorean guns. The superior skill of Baillie's gunners quickly showed and the Mysoreans were forced to abandon many of their cannon during the unequal duel.

Baillie had by this time formed his force into a hollow square formation which advanced steadily onwards in the direction of Conjeveram. Wagons carrying the wounded, the baggage and the ammunition were placed inside the square. Progress was slow as the Mysoreans sent wave after wave of cavalry charging at the square, but disciplined volleys of musket fire, particularly from the 73rd's Grenadier Company, drove the horsemen back time and time again.

Ali, always worried Munro's army would emerge from Conjeveram to attack him in the rear, was on the point of ordering an end to the series of futile cavalry charges when the battlefield was rocked by a massive explosion, followed quickly by a second. A rocket fired by the Mysoreans had hit one of the column's ammunition wagons and set off a chain reaction.

The explosion deprived the British artillery of its ammunition supply and tore a wide gap in the British formation. The Mysorean cavalry charged through the gap in the British lines and began hacking and stabbing at the dazed company sepoys. Baillie realised that his Indian troops were beaten and drew the Highlanders and other European soldiers back to a nearby hillock where they formed a smaller square to repel the Mysorean cavalry. But while an infantry square can stand up to a cavalry charge, it offers an excellent target for cannon. The Mysoreans wheeled up their surviving artillery and began blasting shot into Baillie's tightly packed men. Baillie realised the only way to stop the massacre was to surrender. He tied a white handkerchief to his sword and began waving it as a sign of surrender. In the chaos, it took several minutes for the Mysorean commanders at the scene to realise the British were surrendering. Even then the slaughter did not stop. After the British laid down their muskets, the Mysorean cavalry, many said to be high on drugs, rode into their lines and began cutting the unarmed men down and killing the wounded where they lay.

Lieutenant John Lindsay was carrying a substantial sum of money, intended to buy provisions for his troops during the march, and realised it could be used to buy his life as the enemy cavalry closed in. He picked out one horseman who looked less ferocious than the rest and waved the bag of money at him. The cavalryman not only took the money but also stripped Lindsay to his breeches and shirt. But if Lindsay expected mercy he was mistaken. 'Though much concerned at being thus stripped naked after the part I had acted towards him, I had no doubt but that he would grant me his protection, especially when I saw him mount his horse which he, however, had no sooner done, than he drew his sabre, and, after giving me two or three wounds, instantly rode off, leaving me stung with rage, and laying the blame upon myself for having called him towards me,' Lindsay wrote afterwards.

In the intense heat and suffering from loss of blood, Lindsay fainted and came round to find his shoulder pinned by a pike driven through the body of a soldier lying on top of him. Lindsay was one of those whose lives were saved only by the intervention of Hyder Ali's French advisors who demanded the slaughter of the prisoners should be ended. By that time, Fletcher was dead and Baillie was dying.

Munro had attempted to reach Baillie's beleaguered column after hearing the sound of the cannons firing at Pollilur but it was a half-hearted bid at rescue. The British general abandoned the attempt after meeting some panic-stricken sepoys fleeing the battle who declared all was lost. Munro believed them and threw all his cannon into the water reservoirs at Conjeveram before making a rapid retreat back to Madras.

The 73rd had lost 85 men killed and 127 of its members were dragged off into captivity tied behind the horses of Mysorean cavalrymen. Two wounded soldiers from the regiment managed to escape from the battlefield 'and were later found hiding in some nearby jungle by a British patrol. An estimated 200 European soldiers were dragged to Tipu Sultan's fortress at Seringapatam after the battle. Four years later, when a peace treaty was signed with the Mysoreans, only 30 of them were still alive.

After the battle an unknown number of the East India Company sepoys were also taken to Seringapatam. There they were mistreated and tortured in a bid to persuade them to join the Mysorean Army. The youngest soldiers, white and Indian, were forced to dress up as women and dance for the entertainment of their captors; an estimated 300 of them were forcibly circumcised. The prisoners were held naked or semi-naked and chained in crowded vermin-infested cells. Their diet of rice was mildly toxic and many were slowly poisoned to death. A large number of the men captured had been wounded several times in the battle but they received no medical treatment and their wounds festered for the entire four years they spent in captivity.

One of the 73rd's officers was Captain David Baird. He spent four years with a bullet in his left arm but went on to return to active service after his release from Tipu Sultan's dungeons. He returned to Seringapatam in 1799 and led a force which stormed the fortress. It was Baird who found his old enemy's body lying dead at the bottom of a pile of corpses.

Amongst the plunder captured in 1799 was Tipu Sultan's legendary mechanical tiger. The crudely carved device would simulate eating a redcoated British soldier to the accompaniment of roars and screams generated by a barrel organ hidden inside. In reality, Tipu Sultana had fed the corpses of his dead prisoners to his captive tigers.

A year later, under the more capable and energetic General Sir Eyre Coote, the 73rd was part of an army which inflicted a serious defeat on the Mysorean army near Perambaukum. The march took the British troops through Pollilur where the Highlanders spotted and identified personal belongings of their slain comrades lying scattered and bloodied across the old battlefield.

In 1786 the 73rd was promoted in the list of British Army seniority to the 71st Highlanders. The soldiers were strongly attached to their old number and it took their commander at the time, Lieutenant-Colonel George MacKenzie, armed with loaded pistols, to persuade them to accept their new uniform buttons with the number '71' on them. The 71st eventually became the Highland Light Infantry.

THE WORLD TURNED UPSIDE DOWN

COWPENS 1781

The Fraser Highlanders' misfortunes in the American Revolution did not end in Boston Harbour. During the fighting in the American South, the regiment earned the dubious distinction of being one of the first Highland regiments in the service of the British Crown to run from the enemy. The regiment's 1st battalion was part of a flying column sent to drive rebel Major-General Daniel Morgan and his men into the path of the main British army advancing through South Carolina under Lieutenant-General Charles Cornwallis. The column was commanded by Lieutenant-Colonel Banastre Tarleton, reckoned to be the finest light cavalry commander the British had during the American Revolution. More than 200 years later he was to be immortalised as the psychotic British officer who burned down a church full of villagers in Mel Gibson's movie The Patriot. It did not happen.

The dashing but ruthless Tarleton and his British Legion troops had been a thorn in the side of the rebels for a long time and he was anxious to get the credit for defeating Morgan. The two armies met near the north-west border of South Carolina with its neighbour North Carolina on 17 January 1781, on a semi-cleared grazing ground known locally as Cowpens.

Morgan had chosen a position where the Broad River blocked his only possible retreat. He did this because he had doubts that his 1,600-strong army of militia men and regulars from the rebel

Continental Army would stand up against the determined advance of highly disciplined British troops. But the British Legion was not as well disciplined as Morgan thought and many members of the other units under Tarleton's command were raw recruits. The Highlanders were probably the best of the 1,200-strong British force and they would pay dearly for that in the battle.

Morgan placed his best marksmen, drawn from the South Carolina and Georgia militias, in amongst a thin stand of pine trees which cut across the path of the advancing British troops. He ordered them to fire two volleys at the British when they got within range and then retreat through the lines of regular Continental Army men behind them. The marksmen knew to aim for the British officers and sergeants first. Tarleton's men were tired after an all-night march but he did not give them a chance to catch their breath before advancing straight at the rebels.

The lead was taken by the infantry of the British Legion, men from the 7th Foot and a battalion of light infantry composed of men from several regiments. The militia marksmen fired their two volleys as ordered and then began to pull back. Seeing this, around 60 troopers of the British 17th Light Dragoons charged them but they were counter-charged by 130 rebel cavalry under the command of Lieutenant-Colonel William Washington and driven back; Washington was a cousin of the rebel supreme commander, George Washington.

The rebel musket fire had stalled the British advance and Tarleton sent the Highlanders to swing around the rebels' right flank. As they did so the Continental Army troops began to move back around to face the threat posed by the Highlanders, but in the confusion more men were involved in the manoeuvre than had been intended. The Highlanders, already moving at a jog, quickened their pace in the belief that the rebels had begun to retreat.

But as the Highlanders closed in, the rebels turned around and delivered a withering volley of musket fire at a range of only 30 yards. Around half the Highlanders fell to the ground dead or wounded or, in some cases, in panic. The Highland charge was stalled, but they refused to retreat and held their ground waiting for the rest of the British troops to join them. However, the Highlanders found that the rest of the British infantry was not coming to their aid. The Scots were out on a limb and coming under heavier and heavier fire as more rebels joined the attack on them.

The rebel cavalry under Washington had meanwhile reformed after its successful charge against the British Dragoons and was now heading in the direction of the Highlanders. Tarleton ordered his 200 British Legion cavalry to charge Washington and his men, but instead they turned tail and rode away as fast as their horses would carry them. Tarleton then placed himself at the head of 40 troopers from 7th Light Dragoons and charged Washington's cavalry, but he could only delay the rebel horsemen for so long. The Highlanders were now beginning to retreat in the face of the increasingly heavy rebel musket fire. It did not take long for the withdrawal to turn into a rout and soon the fleeing Highlanders were joined by the rest of the British troops.

The British had lost 210 men killed and a further 710 were captured; there were few British cavalrymen among the prisoners. The rebels lost 150 men killed and wounded.

The only British unit which did not suffer the disgrace of losing its battle colours was the Fraser Highlanders. Their officers blamed Tarleton for the disaster and successfully petitioned Cornwallis never to have to serve under the lieutenant-colonel's command again.

The campaign in the American South took a heavy toll on the health of the British soldiers involved and many suffered from malaria. Both battalions of the Fraser Highlanders were hard hit by disease and after Cowpens it was decided to amalgamate them into one unit.

The Fraser Highlanders were still part of Cornwallis's army when he decided to retreat to the coast at Yorktown. Sadly for Cornwallis, the Highlanders and the rest of the British troops, the

Royal Navy had lost control of the American coast to the French and evacuation from Yorktown was impossible. The recent French intervention in the war meant that by late September 1781, the 6,500 British in Yorktown were surrounded by 9,000 rebels and 7,000 French troops. More important than simple weight of numbers, the French had brought heavy siege guns with them. Defeat was inevitable and on 17 October Cornwallis surrendered. Only about half of his troops were fit enough to march out of the town three days later to lay down their arms as the British military bands played 'The World Turned Upside Down'.

Yorktown was the last major battle of the war. The men of the Fraser Highlanders spent just over a year in captivity before being released when peace was finally agreed in April 1783. The regiment was disbanded at Perth later that year and never reformed.

Yorktown saw the surrender of another Highland regiment which also disbanded at the end of the war. The short-lived Macdonald Highlanders were mustered at Inverness in 1778. Lord Macdonald raised about 750 men from his own estates to fight the rebels and 200 more were recruited in the Lowlands. Another 100 men came from Ireland to make the regiment up to its full strength of just over 1,000.

The regiment arrived in America in 1779 and saw very little action before Yorktown. Briefly, 450 of its men were turned into mounted infantry in an attempt to catch a band of elusive rebels, but the expedition was a failure. Macdonald's men did not see Scotland again until 1784 when the regiment was disbanded at Stirling.

THE TREASURE SEEKERS

BUENOS AIRES 1806

It must have seemed like a good idea at the time. Why not send a battalion of Highlanders to conquer the massive Spanish colony of Rio de la Plata in South America and perhaps grab a little bit of loot in the process? In 1806 the British were on a roll. They had just captured the Dutch colony at the Cape of Good Hope on the southern tip of Africa and Spanish South America looked to some British commanders as yet another easy target for conquest. Both the Dutch and the Spanish were allies of Britain's enemy, Napoleonic France and so their colonies were fair game for attack.

The South American scheme was the brainchild of the Royal Navy commander whose ships had brought the British troops to South Africa, Commodore Home Popham. The Rio de la Plata colony certainly offered a tempting target; it encompassed what are now the countries of Argentina, Paraguay, Uruguay and Bolivia. The colony was rich, but the colonists were said to be unhappy with Spanish rule. Another attraction was that as British trade with Continental Europe was blockaded by the French fleet, Spanish South America could provide a fertile market for British goods if a foothold could be gained there.

Popham had a little problem, however. He had been ordered to keep his ships on the African side of the Atlantic to protect the newly conquered Cape of Good Hope from a counter-invasion. However, he decided that success in South America would override any difficulties from London regarding disobeyed orders. He persuaded the British Army commander in South Africa, Sir David Baird, a survivor of Tipu Sultan's Indian dungeons, to lend him the 71st Highlanders for an expedition which bore more resemblance to a pirate expedition than a military operation. The 71st, Baird's old regiment, was the second-oldest Highland unit in the British army. It had been raised in 1777 by Lord MacLeod, Ian MacKenzie, and contained new fewer than 17 of his clansmen amongst its officers when it was first mustered. By 1806 the regiment was recruiting mainly in Glasgow, which contained a large Highland population who had come south looking for a better life.

The South African campaign had cost the regiment a number of casualties and men from other units were posted in to bring it up to a strength of just under 900 men for the expedition to Rio de la Plata. Popham stopped off at the remote mid-Atlantic island of St Helena where he managed to borrow part of the British garrison for his expedition. Together with the Royal Marines from his own ships, a handful of cavalry dragoons and the 71st, the St Helena troops gave him a force of 1,600 men.

The troops' landing at Quilmes on June 25 was met with little opposition from the Spanish. The British suffered only one casualty as they brushed aside the Spanish force sent to repel the invasion. Most of the best Spanish troops had been sent to the fortress of Montevideo where their commanders had wrongly predicted the British would make their first landing. After two more skirmishes with the Spanish, the British reached Buenos Aires, the biggest and richest city in the colony. As soon as the Spanish Viceroy, the Marquis de Sobremonte, learned of the British invasion, he fled the city with the contents of the colony's treasury loaded onto carts. But the commander of the British troops, Colonel William Beresford, sent some dragoons and men from the 71st mounted on horseback after the Viceroy's convoy and they caught up with it about 40 miles from the city, at the town of Lujan. The carts were carrying over one million Spanish dollars worth of treasure. The loot was quickly put on a ship and sent to

Britain where it was paraded in triumph through the streets of London.

Popham knew that his only chance of avoiding military justice for abandoning his post off the South African coast was to make the money men in London happy. He spent much of his time in Buenos Aires trying to promote British interests and trade. Popham was no stranger to the world of business and when he was younger had briefly left the Royal Navy to go into commercial shipping. That venture fell apart when he was accused of being involved in smuggling and he soon rejoined the navy.

In the early 1800s, the army and navy were also run as businesses, at least as far as the officers were concerned. Army officers could sell jobs and ranks to the highest bidder while naval officers could make small fortunes from their share of the prize money raised from the sale of ships they helped to capture. A similar scheme meant army officers were paid prize money from the proceeds of plunder seized when a city was captured; ordinary soldiers and sailors were also entitled to prize money, but their share was tiny compared with what the officers received. Small wonder then that, after prize money was factored into the equation, the seizure of Buenos Aires seemed an attractive proposition to the senior officers involved.

But the 70,000 citizens of Buenos Aires quickly began turning surly. The population may have had little love for their rulers in Spain, but they saw the British for exactly what they were – not liberators, but invaders. British rule lasted six weeks, then on 10 August, as a fresh Spanish army approached from Montevideo, the population rose against the occupying forces. A small detachment of the 71st stationed near the city's bullring was quickly overwhelmed and massacred. Beresford and the commander of the 71st, Lieutenant-Colonel Denis Pack, tried to lead their men down to Popham's ships in the harbour, but their way was blocked. The city's population pulled hidden muskets from the rafters and cellars of their homes and began sniping at the British from their rooftops. Furniture was thrown from windows and roofs onto the soldiers retreating back into the city centre. The Spanish soldiers from Montevideo and volunteer troops who joined them during their march to Buenos Aires quickly united with the city people in their attack on the British invaders.

The British took shelter in the Santa Domingo Church and the old citadel fortress. The 71st were eventually driven out of the church and, faced with a dwindling stock of food, water and ammunition, and a rising number of wounded, Beresford agreed to surrender the citadel on 12 August. The Spanish commander, Captain Santiago de Liniers agreed that the defeated British would be allowed to march down to Popham's fleet and sail home. However, he was overruled by the city's leading citizens after the surrender and the British were marched off into captivity.

Reinforcements had been sent to join Beresford as soon as news that Buenos Aires had been captured reached South Africa and Britain. But when the fresh troops arrived, they found that the city was back in Spanish hands. Instead of mounting a fresh assault on the city, they sailed to Montevideo and captured it in a bloody battle that cost the British 400 casualties.

The war between the British and Spanish in South America dragged on for another year before the British admitted defeat. The peace deal included the return of the prisoners captured with Beresford at Buenos Aires, but it was soon realised that 35 members of the 71st had deserted by then and joined the Spanish Army. The regiment had lost 91 men killed and wounded during the Buenos Aires campaign, but it was soon up to full strength again. The disaster had not damaged the regiment's reputation and when it was decided to convert some of the best battalions in the British Army into Light Infantry units, the 71st was chosen. The soldiers gave up their kilts to become the Highland Light Infantry.

Beresford and Pack both escaped Spanish custody long before the peace was signed. Officers who gave their word not to escape were given parole and not imprisoned. Pack and Beresford believed their parole status had been revoked by the Spanish when the British captured Montevideo and made their escape. A third officer with them decided not to leave his men behind and remained a prisoner. Pack managed to convince his superiors that he had not broken parole and eventually reached the rank of major-general. He was one of the Duke of Wellington's senior commanders at the Battle of Waterloo.

Beresford also went on to enjoy a successful military career. The Duke of Wellington sent him to train and command the Portuguese Army when it joined the fight against France. He turned out to be a mediocre general, but Wellington recommended him as his successor in the event of his being killed or wounded during the fighting to drive the French out of Spain. Spain had changed sides by this time and Beresford found himself commanding troops who, on the other side of the Atlantic, had once been his enemies.

Popham's career also survived the fiasco of his South American adventure. He was court martialed for leaving South African waters but, as he predicted, the influence of his friends in the financial world ensured that he got off with a reprimand. He was later promoted to the rank of rear admiral.

Santiago de Liniers, who led the Spanish army in South America, was not so lucky. His capture of the 71st led to him being made Viceroy, but in 1809 his French heritage told against him and he was discharged. Like Beresford, he found himself fighting for the Portuguese, but his attempts to put down a rebellion in what is now Brazil ended with his execution in front of a rebel firing squad.

THE WILL OF ALLAH

EL HAMET 1807

Joining the British Army is not usually regarded as a stepping stone to a career in the Turkish civil service or to setting up as a doctor in Egypt. But if Thomas Keith and Donald MacLeod had not joined the 78th Highlanders and half the regiment had not been killed or captured in Egypt in 1806, their lives would undoubtedly have been vastly different. The Turkish Empire in the early 1800s appears to have offered young Scots of humble background more opportunities for advancement than their native land did. Neither man could have had any idea what lay in store for them when they joined the 2nd Battalion of the 78th Highlanders, popularly known as the Ross-shire Buffs.

The battalion was raised by Major-General Alexander Mackenzie-Fraser in 1804 for service against the French who were overrunning Europe under Napoleon. Mackenzie-Fraser's brother-in-law, Lord Seaforth, had raised the regiment's 1st Battalion in 1793 from his estates in the north of Scotland and the surrounding neighbourhoods that still owed allegiance to the Clan MacKenzie.

Recruiters had been scouring the Highlands and Islands for more men since the Napoleonic wars began in 1793 and by 1804 the manpower pool was getting pretty shallow. The 2nd Battalion's ranks were filled with youngsters who were barely more than boys. Questions were asked in high places about how well a battalion in which half the soldiers were under 21 years of age would stand up to the rigours of war.

Many of the battalion's officers were also woefully inexperienced. Several had been made officers simply because they had brought a large number of recruits with them to join the regiment. Lieutenant Christopher Macrae, for example, earned his appointment by bringing 18 of his clansmen with him; six of those men were to die with him in Egypt.

The new battalion's commanding officer, Lieutenant-Colonel Patrick MacLeod, was posted in from the 1st Battalion to give the youngsters some experienced leadership. Officers were also drafted in from the Black Watch and the Rifle Brigade to ensure it had some combat veterans when it went into battle. The Coldstream Guards loaned Major James Macdonnell to the new unit, but few could have even suspected that one day the Duke of Wellington would proclaim him the 'bravest man in England' for his part in holding the key Hougoumont Farm position during the Battle of Waterloo in 1815.

Any doubts about the ability and courage of the inexperienced 2nd Battalion came to an end when they routed a crack battalion of French Grenadiers in Italy during the Battle of Maida in 1806. The young Highlanders went toe-to-toe with the French as the two sides exchanged volleys of musket fire and then launched a charge that swept the grenadiers from the battlefield. MacLeod took a musket ball within an inch of his heart during the battle, but was well enough to resume command of the battalion when it was sent to Egypt in March 1807.

Egypt was nominally part of the Turkish Empire at that time. Control of the country lay in the hands of Albanian troops who had been sent there by the Turks to garrison the country, but who paid little attention to instructions from Constantinople. The warlike Mamelukes who had run Egypt for the Turks before the arrival of the Albanians still held part of the country's south and were scheming to regain total control of it. Both the warring French and British encouraged the Mamelukes' ambitions in a bid to destabilise Egypt.

The British landed with just over 5,000 men and quickly captured the historic port of Alexandria. But it soon became clear that they would also need to gain control of the port of Rosetta 40 miles further east if they were to have a firm foothold in Egypt. A 1,400-strong force was sent to seize Rosetta but it was ambushed as it marched through the narrow streets of the port, with the loss of 185 dead and 282 wounded. The British then decided to lay siege to the port. To protect their besieging army they needed possession of the town of El Hamet on the west bank of the Nile about four miles south of Rosetta. El Hamet not only offered control of the Nile above Rosetta but it also guarded the main road from southern Egypt to the coast.

MacLeod and about 350 of his Highlanders were sent to El Hamet. The force under MacLeod's command also included about 200 men of the Royal Sussex Regiment, 200 German-Swiss mercenaries from De Rolls Regiment and a small force of cavalry from the Chasseurs Britannique, a regiment originally formed from French exiles, but now more of a foreign legion.

MacLeod was told he had permission to abandon El Hamet if attacked by vastly superior forces. He positioned two companies of his own Ross-shire Buffs nearest the river, the men from De Rolls Regiment to hold the village of El Hamet (in the middle of his position) and the men from the Sussex Regiment and the Buffs' Grenadier Company on his right flank. Each position had one cannon assigned to it.

The Albanians attacked on the morning of 21 April. Sentries saw a fleet of 80 boats emerging out of the early morning mist which often hung over the Nile at that time of year. Each boat was packed with bloodthirsty Albanians and, worse still, they were escorted by two small warships armed with cannon. MacLeod decided that these posed a major threat to his troops and ordered a retreat but the men on the right flank were too slow pulling back and a force of Turkish cavalry swept in from the desert to cut them off from the rest of the British force. The Albanians then concentrated on destroying the slow-moving square formation which the three companies from the right flank had by now formed while the British centre and left positions were kept busy holding off the Turkish cavalry.

An officer of the 78th, Major David Stewart, who interviewed survivors of the battle, was later to recount the exploits of one of the men from the square. 'Sergeant John Macrae, a young man, about 22 years of age, but of good size and strength of arm, showed that the broadsword in a firm hand, is as good a weapon in close fighting as the bayonet,' he later wrote.

'If the first push of the bayonet misses its aim, or happens to be parried, it is not easy to recover the weapon and repeat the thrust, when the enemy is bold enough to stand firm; but it is not so with the sword, which may be readily withdrawn from its blow, wielded with celerity, and directed to any part of the body, particularly to the head and arms, whilst its motions defend the person using it.

'Macrae killed six men, cutting them down with his broadsword (of the kind usually worn by sergeants of the Highland corps), when at last he made a dash out of the ranks on a Turk, whom he cut down, but as he was returning to the square he was killed by a blow from behind, his head being split near in two by the stroke of a sabre.

'Thus a lad who, in 1805, was so soft and so childish, displayed in 1807 a courage and vigour worth of a hero of Ossian.'

MacLeod had ridden across the battlefield from his original position on the left to help hurry up the right flank's retreat. He became trapped in the square and was killed before the Albanians finally overran it. Only about two dozen men managed to fight their way out of the square and through the mass of howling Albanian infantry surrounding them in a bid to reach the central position 400 yards away. Most were cut down by the Turkish cavalry before they got very far.

Captain Colin MacKay was amongst the dozen or so Highlanders battling to reach that position. Despite being shot through the thigh, MacKay almost reached the British lines when a Turkish cavalryman took a swing at him with his sword. Only

MacKay's thick cloak and stiff collar stopped the blow taking his head off and two sergeants managed to carry the badly wounded officer into the British position.

MacKay was placed under the carriage of a cannon and lay there urging the troops to fight to the last bullet rather than surrender. After the battle it was said by another officer of the 78th, who was not present, that the Albanian commander presented MacKay with his sword to honour the Scot's bravery.

By now the Highlanders who had been stationed closest to the river had managed to join the men of the De Rolls Regiment in the centre position and they formed a square to hold off the Albanian infantry and Turkish cavalry who now surrounded them on all sides. Some of the surviving officers wanted to begin moving the square in the direction of Rosetta, but the soldiers refused to leave the wounded to the mercy of the enemy. However, ammunition was running low and the Albanians were wheeling up a captured six-pounder cannon which would devastate the tightly packed ranks of British survivors if it opened fire. The British had no choice but to surrender.

There was chaos as the Albanians and Turks, along with some Arab troops, fought with each other in the rush to grab a British prisoner as every man who handed over a prisoner was entitled to a reward of seven dollars. Other members of the victorious army began hacking the heads off the dead British soldiers for display in Cairo. Some Turkish cavalrymen galloped around the battlefield with severed heads on the ends of their lances.

Around 400 British soldiers were captured and some of them were forced to carry bags containing the heads of 300 or so dead down to the river where a fleet of boats was waiting to take them to Cairo. The living were paraded through the city several times in triumph before being locked up in the dungeons of the citadel while the heads of the dead were put on public display. MacLeod's head was given pride of place.

The 78th had lost 163 men killed at El Hamet while the total enemy loss has been estimated at around 1,000. The men captured were released five months later when the British agreed to leave Egypt. Two men, Private Thomas Keith and Drummer Donald MacLeod, did not return home; both converted to Islam and stayed put. MacLeod, one of the 200 young men from Lewis who had joined the 2nd Battalion, changed his name to Osman and, following a brief period of slavery, set himself up as a doctor. His way with leeches earned him fame and fortune in Cairo despite his previous medical experience being limited to helping the 2nd Battalion's doctor mix medicines and roll bandages.

Keith did even better. He had joined the battalion after a period spent as an apprentice gunsmith in Leith. He put his skills as an armourer at the disposal of the Turks and took the name Ibrahim Aga. He proved an able soldier in Turkish service and was promoted to the rank of general in the cavalry. At the age of 26 he was made governor of the Islamic holy city of Medina, the last resting place of the Prophet Mohammed. This appointment, a reward for being the first soldier into the city when the Turks stormed it, lasted only a few months. Keith died shortly before his 30th birthday in a cavalry skirmish sometime in 1815.

THE STONEWALL HIGHLANDERS

NEW ORLEANS 1815

As the stationary redcoated ranks of the 93rd Sutherland Highlanders were torn open by cannon and musket fire from the American troops hidden safe behind their stockade, none of them knew that the war had been over for two weeks. The Highlanders had been sent to Louisiana in late 1814 as part of a force which was to capture the port of New Orleans during the war between the United States and Britain which had broken out two years before. The Americans had long regretted their failure to seize Canada during the American Revolution and saw the war going on in Europe between Britain and Napoleonic France as an excellent opportunity for a second attempt.

The unashamedly expansionist United States Government invaded Canada in 1812 on the pretext that the British had been interfering with American ships as part of their blockade of France. The war in Europe meant the British could spare few troops to defend Canada, but despite this the Americans were held at bay for two years by a handful of redcoats, Indians and Canadian militiamen.

The defeat of Napoleon in 1814 meant that the British were finally in a position to send enough troops to Canada for a meaningful offensive against the Americans. Many of those British soldiers had been living off American grain, supplied through Portuguese middlemen, while fighting the French. The Americans never let war interfere with business.

British troops mounted a seaborne raid on Washington which brushed aside a poorly organised American army sent to protect the US capital. The British then burned all the public buildings in the city. The raid was in revenge for a similar outrage against what is now the Canadian city of Toronto committed by the Americans earlier in the war. The White House got its name because it had to be whitewashed to hide the scorch marks.

But Britain's admirals had their eyes on a richer target than Washington; the port of New Orleans had been sold by France with the rest of Louisiana to the United States in 1803. Its docks and warehouses were stacked with of cotton and tobacco awaiting export and worth three million pounds. It has to be explained that in the early 1800s the British paid their soldiers and sailors prize money for captured enemy property. The cash came from the sale of the plunder and was distributed according to rank, with the lion's share going to the senior officers. There can be little doubt that prize money was the main motive for the attack on New Orleans.

A British fleet infiltrated the network of rivers and lagoons which make up southern Louisiana and deposited a small British army within six-days' hard rowing of New Orleans. If the British had headed for the city straight away, they would undoubtedly have captured it before the Americans had time to complete their defences. Instead, the cautious British commander, Major-General John Keane, decided to wait for reinforcements first; when he finally decided he had enough men, he set off to row to New Orleans. His soldiers spent a miserable time, pounded all the way by torrential rain, negotiating a swampy river which eventually brought them to within six miles of New Orleans.

It was at this point that the British found US General Andrew Jackson and his men waiting for them behind a mile-long stockade anchored at one end by an impassable swamp and on the other by the mighty Mississippi River. The stockade was built of cotton bales and wooden casks filled with sugar and could easily withstand the pounding of the small cannon the British had brought with them in their boats. Furthermore, the Americans did not have the same transport problems as the British and had hauled up 24 heavy cannon to help defend the stockade. These out-ranged most of the British guns and made any effective bombardment of the stockade impossible.

By this time the British had a new commanding officer. He was Major-General Sir Edward Packenham, a brother-in-law of the top British general at the time, the Duke of Wellington. The Iron Duke referred to Packenham as 'not exactly the brightest genius,' but acknowledged that he was one of the more competent generals the British had at the time. Packenham was well known in the British army at the time for a rather strange disability he once had. A spent bullet had hit him in the neck in 1813 and gave his head a decided tilt to one side; when he was hit by another spent bullet on the other side of his neck a few months later, the tilt vanished.

Packenham realised that as his artillery was ineffective against the stockade, it would have to be stormed at bayonet point. Previous British experience fighting the Americans suggested that they would flee in the face of a determined advance by veterans of the recent war in Europe. One of the key positions in the American defences was actually on the far bank of the Mississippi. The Americans had set up a battery of cannon which could fire across the river into the flank of any force trying to storm the stockade. Packenham decided these guns would have to be silenced before the main attack was made on the morning of 8 January 1815.

The plan to deal with the battery involved sending a force of troops under the command of Colonel William Thornton across the river in boats to storm it. But this meant cutting a canal through the bank of the Mississippi for the assault boats and the British engineers miscalculated. When the earth was removed to complete the canal, it drained into the Mississippi and left the boats high and dry.

However, Thornton managed to get about a third of his men across the river just before Packenham's attack on the stockade was scheduled to begin and they successfully routed the American gunners. Packenham, however, had already run into more problems. Troops from the 44th East Essex regiment had been detailed to lead the assault and had been told to take scaling ladders with them to get over the stockade. The unit had suffered heavy casualties in Europe and had been heavily reinforced with raw recruits before sailing for America. For some reason, they forgot the ladders and had to be sent back to get them.

The whole assault plan was thrown into chaos and as the sun rose the British were still not ready to advance. As the Americans could see an attack was imminent and were expected to start pounding the British with their cannon at any moment, it was decided to launch the attack anyway.

As the East Essex were still fetching their ladders, the brunt of the responsibility for the assault now fell on the 21st Royal Scots Fusiliers and the 4th King's Own Royal Lancaster Regiment. The Fusiliers were regarded at the time as a strong battalion but its men were thought of as sulky and undisciplined. Most of their best troops had been siphoned off with the flank companies of the other regiments to form an elite Light Battalion which was to storm a battery of cannon in a small fort at the end of the stockade closest to the river.

The Fusiliers advanced steadily, protected from the fire of the Americans by an outcrop of trees. About 100 yards from the stockade they came out of the cover of the trees and, as they quickened their pace, they were met by a storm of musket, cannon and rifle fire. Marksmen from the 95th Rifles opened fire to keep the heads of the American riflemen down, but the cannon mounted along the stockade and firing oversized buckshot took a heavy toll on the attackers.

One of the Fusiliers, Lieutenant John Leavock, managed to scramble over the stockade; he was greeted by the sight of the Americans running for their lives. Only two Americans, both officers, stood their ground ahead of him. However, as Leavock looked around he had an unpleasant surprise. He was alone.

'Conceive my indignation on looking round to find that the two leading regiments had vanished as if the earth had opened and swallowed them,' he was to write afterwards.

The rest of the Fusiliers had either already retreated or were hugging the ground in front of the stockade to duck the hail of lead coming from it. The Lancasters were not making any progress either. Leavock, already wounded in two earlier skirmishes with the Americans, was quickly captured as the Americans flocked back to their posts in the realisation that he had no back-up.

The Americans were keeping their heads down behind the stockade and most of their musket fire was going over the heads of the British, but the redcoats were also firing wildly. Soon British soldiers began streaming towards the rear. Packenham was particularly appalled by the conduct of the East Essex and cried out to them as they passed, 'For Shame! Recollect that you are British soldiers'; but his shouts did little to stem the tide and minutes later while still trying to rally his troops he was shot dead. He had already been wounded twice during the battle.

Meanwhile, on the other side of the battlefield, closest to the river, the Sutherland Highlanders were marching in tightly packed ranks towards the stockade. Before the advance began, around 90 of them sank to their knees in prayer. The regiment was a magnificent sight in its tartan trews and redcoats.

The Americans let them get to within about 150 yards of the stockade before unleashing a withering hail of fire which cut down a number of the Highlanders, including their commanding officer, Lieutenant-Colonel Dale. His death led to confusion in the ranks. Dale had been told to attack either the river end of the stockade or its centre portion, 'according to circumstances'.

The Highlanders were within a minute of reaching the stockade when their new acting commander called them to a halt. He then refused to advance or retreat until he had found out what the 'circumstances' demanded of the Highlanders were. By this time, the Light Battalion had succeeded in storming the fort at the river end of the stockade and if the Highlanders had joined them, the battle might have been won.

Instead, while new orders were sought, the Highlanders stood rock-still 100 yards from the stockade. One American said they were as 'firm and immovable as a brick wall'. It was a magnificent display of discipline and courage, but the muskets and cannon behind the stockade were ripping great holes in their ranks. Every time men in the front line fell, mangled and torn by the storm of lead, more Highlanders stepped up to take their places.

A British officer shouted at the Highlanders, 'Ninety-third, have a little patience, and you shall have your revenge'. But it was not to be. With Packenham dead and most of the British troops now retreating, the Highlanders were ordered to withdraw. Not a single man in the main Highland attack had seen an American.

The Light Battalion, which included 100 men from the Sutherland Highlanders, were also forced to retreat. Once out of range of the American cannon, the British halted and camped for 10 days within sight of the stockade. Then they began the retreat back to the coast. Heavy winter rains meant that many of the men sank up to their thighs in the heavy gumbo mud during the march.

In those days a number of soldiers' wives were allowed to travel with their husbands to war. When the wives spotted the boats bringing the retreating army back out of the Louisiana swamps, they set out to meet the convoy. The Highlanders' wives had the sympathy of the convoy. Fifty-six members of the regiment had died in front of the stockade and a further 21 of the 380 listed as wounded when roll call was taken after the battle were also dead. Wounds had also claimed the lives of 39 out of the 121 Highlanders captured by the Americans.

The Highlanders had landed in Louisiana with 985 men. The Royal Scots Fusiliers left behind 70 dead and 331 prisoners from a total of 800 men involved in the assault on the stockade. The battalion also recorded 114 wounded. In total, the British lost 266 men killed and 1,126 wounded while the Americans recorded 13 dead and 39 wounded. The Americans also listed 71 men as missing.

The losses that the Sutherland Highlanders suffered at New Orleans meant the regiment played no further part in the campaign. The Fusiliers went on to help capture the main fort protecting the city of Mobile before news finally reached the British that a peace agreement had been signed on December 24 the previous year.

The peace treaty was basically a return to the status quo before the Americans invaded Canada and meant the British had to return Detroit which they had captured early on in the war. The British prisoners were released on 26 February – minus their boots and shoes, which had been stolen by their American captors – and were soon sailing for home.

General Jackson went on to become US president and it was a long time before the Americans seriously considered invading Canada again. More than 140 of the Highlanders who survived the Battle of New Orleans were judged too badly injured for further military service and were discharged from the army. Many found they had no homes to return to. The regiment recruited heavily in Caithness and Sutherland where the Highland Clearances were now in full swing. The disabled veterans arrived in the north of Scotland to find their families had been evicted by landlords who wanted the land for sheep farming. Having nearly lost their lives in the service of king and country, they returned to find they had little left to show for their loyalty.

SCOTLAND FOREVER!

WATERLOO 1815

There cannot be many army units which mark one of their worst disasters by commemorating it on their cap badge. That, however, is just what the Royal Scots Dragoon Guards do. The Waterloo Eagle on their badge recalls the day the regiment was almost wiped out in a charge that went on too long.

The regiment was then known officially as the Royal North British Dragoons, but everyone knew them as the Scots Greys, because of the massive grey chargers they rode into battle; they were also easily distinguished on the battlefield because of their bearskin headgear. The Scots Greys were heavy cavalry, which meant that they relied on sheer momentum to smash through enemy forma-tions. Certainly, their heavy cavalry swords were not much help. The sabres were made of poor quality metal and were easily blunted. Unless used in expert hands, they were more likely to bludgeon an enemy's skull than cleave it.

The British commander at Waterloo, the legendary Duke of Wellington, had little faith in his cavalry. 'Our cavalry has never gained a battle yet,' he wrote. 'When the infantry have beaten the French, then the cavalry, if they can act, make the whole complete, and do wonders, but they have never yet beaten the French themselves.'

The cavalry were amongst the worst offenders in the British Army when it came to measuring an officer's worth in terms of his personal wealth rather than on battlefield ability and performance. Wellington knew only too well that once unleashed in a charge, his cavalry were out of the battle for the rest of day. The cavalry officers were unable to control their men once the charge had begun and could not get them to reform their ranks for further battle.

When the French dictator Napoleon escaped from exile in 1815 and restarted the war which had been ravaging Europe almost constantly since 1792 much of the British Army was still in America after helping repulse an invasion of Canada. Wellington had very few veterans to fight Napoleon's French. However, several of his most experienced units were Scots ones who had fought under his command in Spain and Portugal. He brought five them together and placed them in the centre of his defensive positions on the ridge near Waterloo, under the command of Lieutenant-General Thomas Picton. Two of the veteran units, the Black Watch and the Gordon Highlanders, had suffered heavy casualties two days earlier when they stopped the French driving a wedge between Wellington's army and the Prussian Army. Napoleon knew that if the two armies combined they would outnumber his own troops. He wrongly believed that the Prussian Army had been defeated by his troops two days earlier and that he now had a free hand to deal with Wellington's ramshackle force of mainly raw British recruits and Dutch, German and Belgian troops. The Scots in the centre were supported by three regiments of heavy cavalry, the Scots Greys, the Irishmen of the Iniskilling Dragoons and the English Royal Dragoons; the cavalry force was called the Union Brigade because it brought together troopers from England, Scotland and Ireland.

Napoleon opened the battle around 11am when he sent a strong force under his brother Jerome to capture the fortified farmhouse at Hougoumont at the bottom of the valley which separated the two armies. The farm was on the right side of the battlefield and the Scots were spectators to the fierce fighting for possession of it.

Then at around 2pm the French troops opposite the Scots began marching towards them. The French drums pounded out a steady heavy beat as the columns of French plodded forward, 15,000 bayonets glinting in the afternoon sun. The skirl of the Highlanders' pipers was heard in answer as the Scots moved forward to a hedge near the valley bottom. A force of Belgian troops, who had a reputation as brave fighters but whose hearts were not in this battle, broke and ran before the French reached them. The 3,000 British troops in the centre jeered and booed at the fleeing Belgians. Some of the British soldiers wanted to shoot at the Belgians, but were stopped by their officers.

About 100 feet from the hedge, the French came to halt in the clawing mud of the valley bottom and prepared to launch themselves at the Scots. Just then the Black Watch, the Gordons and Royal Scots unleashed a devastating volley of musket fire. Then with a roar they charged at the French with their bayonets waving. The Gordon's pipers played 'Johnnie Cope' as the Highlanders ran at the French.

It was then that the Scots Greys rode through the Gordons to get at the French, knocking several of them to the ground. Some of the Gordons, recruited from the Duke of Gordon's Highland estates, which ran deep into Inverness-shire, managed to grab the stirrups of the cavalry troopers and were carried for a few giant-sized bounds towards the French. The cry 'Scotland Forever' was heard over the din of battle.

The speed and momentum of that the charge has long been disputed and may have been nothing more than a fast trot, but the shock value of it was enough to send the French reeling. The volley of musket fire unleashed earlier by the Scots infantry had created a thick cloud of smoke which still clung to the valley bottom as the Greys emerged from it to surprise the leading French troops.

The brunt of the Grey's charge was taken by the French 45th Regiment of the Line, which was composed of youngsters from the slums of Paris. It was against them that the Greys' giant of a fencing instructor, 45-year-old Sergeant Charles Ewart, showed what could be done with a heavy cavalry sabre in expert hands. He made for the spot where the prestigious Eagle standard of the 45th Regiment of the Line was being waved to rally its members.

About six men were defending the Eagle. Ewart, whose exploits made him a national hero, later recounted, 'One made a thrust at my groin. I parried it off and cut him through the head. A lancer came at me – I threw the lance off to my right side and cut him through the chin and upwards through the teeth. Next a foot soldier fired at me, and then charged me with his bayonet, which I also had the good luck to parry, and then cut him through the head.' Ewart seized the Eagle, an action commemorated on the regiment's cap badge to this day, and was ordered by no less a person than the Union Brigade's commander himself, Sir William Ponsonby, to carry it back to the British lines.

All may have been well if the rest of the Greys had gone back with him, but as Ewart unwillingly turned his back on the fighting the rest of the regiment plunged onwards after the fleeing French. Bloodlust shone in the eyes of the troopers as they chased after the French. Not all the French columns had been broken by the Union Brigade's charge and many of the men in them opened fire on the cavalry troopers as they rode past in pursuit of the running men. However, the reckless charge led the French to believe they faced more British cavalry than they actually did and the intact columns began to retreat as well.

The Greys' commanding officer, Lieutenant-Colonel James Hamilton, was seen riding with the reins of his horse gripped in his teeth after being wounded in both hands. He was later found among the dead with both arms cut off. Hamilton is said to have tried to rally his men and get them back to the British lines. Even if the troopers had wanted to stop the charge, the horses did not; the Greys charged on and got into a French artillery position. There they began chasing the gunners, many no more than boys, and hacking at them as they tried to dodge between the guns.

But the Greys were now a spent force. Those who looked behind them would have seen the glinting steel breastplates of a large force of French Cuirassiers who were riding their horse down into the valley to cut the British cavalry off. Alongside the Cuirassiers were the agile and lightly-equipped Lancers, the tips of their weapons sparkling in the sun.

The Greys started urging their tired horses back towards the British-held ridge on the other side of the valley. But the scattered groups of horsemen were too slow to outrun the Lancers on their fresh horses and the redcoated troopers were picked off in ones and twos by the Lancers. The Greys fought hard with swords and even hands to fend off the thrusting lances, but they were too heavily outnumbered to have much chance of making it back to the British lines.

When the survivors of the charge mustered back behind the British front line there were barely 40 Greys to answer the roll call. More men drifted back over the rest of the afternoon but out of approximately 350 troopers who charged with the regiment, over 100 were dead and another 100 were wounded; the usual ratio of wounded to dead is closer to three-to-one. For the Greys, the Battle of Waterloo was effectively over. Their charge led some French soldiers to speculate they were all drunk. When Napoleon ordered his Cuirassiers and Lancers to wipe out the Greys, he had marvelled at the courage of the Scots cavalry: 'Ces terribles chevaux gris'; although 'gris' in French can mean drunk or grey. Scots units lost just over 400 dead at Waterloo, with the Greys making up a quarter of the total.

Back in the valley and up the slope towards the main French positions, the ground was scattered with British and French dead. Perhaps the saddest sights of all were the badly wounded horses struggling in the thick mud to get back on their feet as their wide eyes rolled in panic. In other spots rider-less horses stood calmly chomping at the grass and ignored the battle still going on around them as the French massed for yet another attack on the British.

The battle raged all day, but the French failed to push the British off their ridge before the Prussian Army arrived to clinch victory for the allies. A general advance was ordered and the surviving Greys nudged their mounts into a slow walk across the battlefield. A battle which would decide the shape of Europe for almost 100 years had been won, but few of the Scots troopers were in any shape to celebrate.

WOMEN AND CHILDREN FIRST

THE *BIRKENHEAD* 1852

Death in battle was often the least of a soldier's worries in the past. Poor medical services meant that disease frequently took a heavy toll on troops sent overseas. One posting to India in 1845 cost the 78th Highlanders 498 men dead from cholera; the same outbreak also killed 171 of their wives and children. Transportation was far from hazard-free and regimental histories are dotted with accounts of shipwrecks.

One of the worst was the sinking of the troopship HMS *Birkenhead* off the South African coast in February 1852. The events of that dreadful night were to inspire generations of Victorian schoolboys and encourage the notion that women and children should get priority when it came to lifeboats. School text books and other 'improving literature' often carried illustrations of steadfast ranks of redcoats standing to attention on the tilted deck of a ship which was rapidly sinking below their feet.

All 31 children and 25 women on board the *Birkenhead* survived the sinking, but almost 450 soldiers and sailors drowned rather than risk swamping the three available lifeboats. The ship had been carrying 638 passengers and crew when it sank. Most of the soldiers were new recruits and many were teenagers.

The 73rd Highlanders, later to become the 2nd Black Watch, suffered worst in the tragedy; out of 73 members of the regiment on board the *Birkenhead*, 56 were drowned. The 74th Highlanders, later the 2nd Highland Light Infantry, were also hard hit, with 50 dead out of 63 on board. The 91st Argyllshire Regiment, who became the 1st Argyll and Sutherland Highlanders, lost 45 of its contingent of 103.

The *Birkenhead*, a paddle steamer, had been carrying reinforcements from Britain to South Africa for regiments fighting to put down a revolt by Kaffir tribesmen. As well as the drafts for the Scottish regiments, the ship was also carrying members of the 12th Lancers, the 2nd Foot, the 6th Foot, the 12th Foot, the 43rd Foot, the 45th Foot and the King's Royal Rifle Corps.

Few people were on the deck when the *Birkenhead* ran at full cruising speed onto a jagged tooth of rock sticking out of the sea off the aptly named Danger Point around 2am on 25 February. The first that many of the soldiers – packed like sardines below decks in their hammocks – knew of the disaster was the sound of the hull being ripped open and water pouring into the holds. No-one will ever know how many men were drowned before they could scramble up onto the main deck and fresh air. The soldiers pushed, pulled and shoved as they fought their way up the ladders out of the holds. Few were in uniform, most were half-dressed, some were still naked.

On deck they were met by the officers who were travelling with them to South Africa. Discipline was enforced and the chaos subsided. Around 50 soldiers were ordered back below deck to help man the ship's pumps. The other surviving soldiers were lined up in ranks on the deck and ordered to remain still until all the women and children were put in lifeboats. However, it was quickly realised that there would be very few spaces left on the lifeboats once the women and children were embarked.

The wood on some of the other lifeboats was so rotten that it disintegrated as the sailors tried to launch them. Other lifeboats could not be launched at all because the pulleys intended to lower them into the water were jammed or even painted solid. In the end only two of the ship's cutters and a smaller gig were actually launched. Several horses which had been on board were pushed into the water in the hope they would be able to swim to shore two miles away.

At this point the ship's captain, Robert Salmond, made a serious mistake by trying to reverse the *Birkenhead* off the rock. The manoeuvre increased the size of the rip in her hull and more water cascaded in and flooded the engine room. Almost all the soldiers who had been sent to man the pumps were drowned and the ship then split in two. Salmond then gave the order to abandon ship. However, the senior British officer on board, Lieutenant-Colonel Alexander Seton of the 74th Highlanders, ordered the men on deck to stand steady rather than risk swamping the lifeboats.

'I implore you not to do this thing, and I ask you to stand fast,' he said. Survivors said afterwards that following Seaton's intervention the men went completely silent. Several soldiers then turned to men who had only been their comrades for a few short weeks and solemnly shook hands with them. All knew that their chances of survival if they tried to swim in the shark-infested water were slim. The shouts of the wives to the soldiers on deck and the wailing of children for their fathers only made the ordeal worse.

Only 20 minutes after first hitting the rock, the *Birkenhead* slid under the water. The only part of the ship to be seen above the sea was a section of the mainmast; soldiers were clinging to the rigging like flies. Other soldiers swam away from the ship and grabbed onto pieces of wreckage now bobbing around in the water.

It was not long until the sharks started feeding. The first to be pulled under were the men who had gone into the water naked; the sharks probably mistaking them for seals, their usual prey. Gradually more and more men were dragged under by the sharks. The number of men in the water increased as the strength of those clinging to what remained of the mainmast gave out and they plunged from the rigging.

One man who had looked certain to survive the ordeal was 19-year-old Ensign Alexander Russell of the 74th Highlanders. He had been assigned a place in one of the lifeboats with the women and children, but when one of those women recognised her husband in the water, Russell gave up his place on the boat for him. Russell then began to swim behind the boat, but five minutes later he was pulled under by a shark.

Some soldiers did manage to swim ashore and some non-swimmers were lucky enough to be washed up alive on shore. As dawn broke, a passing ship, the *Lioness*, came across one of the lifeboats and immediately after picking up its occupants, headed for the spot where the *Birkenhead* had sunk. She arrived to find 50 men still clinging to the jutting mainmast. After rescuing them, the ship went on to pick up the few remaining men in the water.

The courage of the soldiers, nearly all teenage recruits, became the stuff of legend for Victorian Britons. Captain Edward Wright of the 91st Highlanders survived the sinking and was honoured for his part in steadying the troops after the ship first hit the rock. He was full of praise for the young mens' courage.

'Orders were carried out as if the men were embarking instead of going to the bottom,' he wrote afterwards. 'There was only this difference, that I never saw an embarkation conducted with so little noise and confusion.'

The greatest living English soldier of the time, the Duke of Wellington, made one of his last public appearances before his death to praise the redcoats' discipline and award Wright a pension of £100 pounds a year. Another survivor, Corporal W Smith, wrote years later to explain why the men stood firm on the deck that terrible night.

'The British soldier's duty was to obey every order, without wondering, as they do nowadays, why it was given and whether it was right,' he wrote some years later. 'They were days of iron discipline and not overmuch consideration for the private soldier, who was still only a machine for fighting purposes.

'Does not panic die away at the word of command?

'And why? Because there are women and children on board, and the women and children are to be saved, whatever happens to the rest.'

Some witnesses reported that after the men were ordered to

stand firm on deck, Seton and Salmond clambered into a lifeboat which they ordered lowered into the water. However, the boat was so rotten that it disintegrated under their feet and they plunged to their deaths in the water.

The story took another twist when rumours began to circulate that the *Birkenhead* was carrying £240,000 worth of gold bullion which was to be used to pay the British army in South Africa. It was not long before salvage attempts were begun, but despite repeated searches over the past 150 years, the gold has never been found.

WALPOLE'S FOLLY

RUIYA 1858

General Sir Robert Walpole's life was in a danger – but the threat came from his own men. Highland soldiers were so outraged by Walpole's blundering attack on a jungle fort in north-eastern India that they wanted to kill the general who had so senselessly thrown away their comrades' lives. Amongst those killed in the botched assault on an isolated fort at Ruiya during the Indian Mutiny in the late 1850s was one of the most popular and promising young Scottish officers in the British Army, Adrian Hope of the Sutherland Highlanders.

Glaswegian Lieutenant-General Sir Colin Campbell had entrusted Walpole with the pride of his army – The Highland Brigade. Walpole's force was built around three Highland regiments, the Black Watch, the Cameron Highlanders and the Sutherland Highlanders. Both the Black Watch and the Sutherland Highlanders had distinguished themselves weeks earlier during the bloody capture of the Indian city of Lucknow in February 1858 from the mutinous Indian troops and local rebels; the two regiments had served under Campbell during the Crimean War only three years before and the Sutherland Highlanders had been immortalised during that conflict as the original 'Thin Red Line' by *The Times* war correspondent William Russell.*

---

* Russell actually described the Highlanders as a 'thin red streak' defying the masses of Russian cavalry on the plain that led to the British-held port of Balaclava; but most people remembered the phrase as 'thin red line'.

The fighting at Lucknow had been brutal and no mercy was shown to the defeated Indian troops. They were massacred on the spot by British soldiers enraged by stories of atrocities committed against white families who had fallen into the hands of the rebels. The murder of 200 women and children who had been promised safe passage after the surrender of the British garrison at Cawnpore was said to be the justification for the massacre of the entire 2,000-strong rebel garrison of one of the main strongpoints in Lucknow.

The Indian Mutiny broke out in May 1857 and took more than two years to suppress. The process was bloody. Captured mutineers were tied to cannon and blasted to smithereens. Groves of trees in villages suspected of being in sympathy with the rebels hung heavy with their dangling bodies after British columns had marched through them.

Britain had been slowly taking over the Indian sub-continent province by province for over 100 years before the mutiny. Some territories were annexed outright, while the rulers of others became British puppets in return for a generous pension. The process had been accelerated in the 1850s by the Governor-General Lord Dalhousie. The crunch came when Dalhousie announced that as there was no heir to the throne of the Kingdom of Oudh, which included the strategically important Upper Ganges Valley in north-eastern India, it was being annexed. A year later, the simmering discontent of many Indians flared into mutiny and rebellion. Most of the Indian troops serving in north-eastern India with the Bengal Army came from Oudh and proved easy prey for political agitators.

The spark came when the Indian soldiers of the Bengal Army were issued with new rifles which used greased cartridges. The grease was made from animal fat and both Hindu and Muslim soldiers refused to use them on religious grounds. Before the situation could be defused, the Indian troops at Meerut mutinied. White officers and their families were massacred and British garrisons across India were besieged.

British troops, many fresh from fighting in the Crimean War, which had just ended, flooded into India and Indian troops loyal to the British from the Madras and Bombay armies were brought in to help suppress the rebellion. In Oudh the mutineers were joined by local rebels who resented the British annexation of the kingdom. The kingdom quickly became the main focus for rebel activity in India.

The small British garrison in Lucknow, the old capital of Oudh, found itself under siege in late May 1857 and, along with some Indian troops who remained loyal, held the government compound against a rebel force which at times numbered more than 50,000 men. A relief force under Major-General Henry Havelock arrived in September but was too small to drive the rebels out of the city; it found itself joining the original garrison in defending the government compound.

In November, General Campbell, the son of a Glasgow cabinetmaker, broke the siege and evacuated both the garrison and the first relief force to safety. In late February 1858 Campbell returned with the largest British army so far fielded against the rebels, 30,000 men, and retook the city in two weeks of bitter and bloody street fighting.

Those rebels who had managed to escape the slaughter at Lucknow were gathering near Bareilly about 170 miles north-west of the city to continue the fight. Campbell decided to split his army into four columns which were ordered to converge on Bareilly for a final, and hopefully decisive, showdown with the rebels. The Scottish general believed the columns would face only a few isolated pockets of resistance which could be easily overcome.

Walpole was a well-known blunderer, but, because he was one of the most senior officers at Lucknow, Campbell was forced by War Office protocol to make him a column commander. To deal with any rebels in Walpole's path, Campbell entrusted him with his beloved Highlanders and one of his best young officers, Brigadier Adrian Hope. In an army where length of service counted for more than ability when it came to rank, Hope had risen to the command of the Highland Brigade at the comparatively young age of 37.

After his death, Campbell wrote that, 'The death of this most distinguished and gallant officer causes the deepest grief to the Commander in Chief.

'Still young in years, he had risen to high command and by his undaunted courage, combined as it was with extreme kindness and charm of manner, had secured the confidence of the brigade in no ordinary degree.'

War correspondent Russell was even more fulsome in his praise of Hope.

'A gentler, braver spirit never breathed – a true soldier, a kind courteous, noble gentleman, in word and deed; devoted to his profession, beloved by his men, adored by his friends – this is indeed a sad loss to the British army.'

The Highland troops were glad to leave Lucknow behind. The ruined city strongly resembled a slaughterhouse. There were piles of rebel bodies rotting in the heat of the Indian summer and thick black clouds of flies hovered over lakes of blood in the streets. Temperatures over 100° Fahrenheit were being recorded in the shade.

The Highlanders were joined on their march by the Sikhs of the 4th Punjab Infantry, the British 9th Lancers, the 2nd Punjab Cavalry and 18 cannon. In all, Walpole had a formidable force of 6,000 men. Campbell issued specific orders that no rebel forts were to be assaulted without artillery support. The rebels, in turn, had been ordered by their leaders not to fight any open battles with the British. Instead, they were to harass the advancing British troops by attacking their supply columns.

Walpole's column left Lucknow on 7 April 1858. The heat was intense and the route of the march took the troops through an area of thick jungle with few roads. It took seven days to march the 51 miles from Lucknow to the mud-walled stronghold of rebel chieftain Nirpat Singh at Riuya.

Singh was reputed to be a fair-weather rebel with no stomach for a fight with the British. A man who turned up at Walpole's camp, claiming to have escaped from imprisonment at Riuya, said that Singh would offer only token resistance to maintain his honour before surrendering.

Walpole refused to believe the man and ordered a frontal assault on the stronghold. He neither waited for his artillery nor carried out a reconnaissance. A reconnaissance would have revealed the attack was being launched against the strongest part of the fort. The walls on the east and south sides of the stronghold were so low that a man could easily have jumped over them and the adjoining jungle would have provided cover for the British if they had launched their assault on these walls.

Instead, Walpole ordered four companies of the Black Watch to attack across the open ground in front of the fort where the wall was highest and a protective ditch had been dug. Between the ditch and the wall was a thicket of brush and bamboo which acted as a natural barbed-wire entanglement. The 200 or so defenders could not believe what they were seeing as the Highlanders emerged from the jungle into the clearing in front of the ditch. They opened fire with the muskets and cannon on the closely packed ranks of British troops.

The Black Watch's advance ended abruptly when they reached the ditch. The ditch was a surprise and the Highlanders sent messengers back to request ladders to help them get across it and then to scale the stronghold wall. Instead the 4th Punjabs swept into the attack and were mown down by a hail of musket fire and cannon balls from the fort. With the frontal attack stalled, Walpole now brought up his artillery. However, many of the cannon balls flew over the fort and landed among the Highlanders.

Hope, who had command of all three Highland regiments, had protested against the frontal assault. He now went forward to see for himself what was going on and was shot dead through the chest by a sniper perched in the branches of a tree growing inside the fort.

Sergeant William Forbes-Mitchell was part of a party of Sutherland Highlanders providing cover for a British officer sent into the jungle to find an alternative way into the fort. He said afterwards that he believed Hope had been shot by a renegade British soldier who had joined the rebels in the opening days of the mutiny.

He said from his position in the jungle that he could clearly hear a man shouting from the tree in barrack-room English at the Highlanders lining the ditch and daring them to continue their assault, 'Come on, you fuckin' Highlanders! Come on, Scotty! You have a harder nut to crack than eating oatmeal porridge. If you can come through these bamboos we'll warm your balls for you if you come in here.'

Forbes-Mitchell said it was this renegade who persuaded Singh to defend the fort properly. Years later the sergeant met an old mutineer who told him that the renegade had been a sergeant-major in an Indian regiment which had mutinied and murdered its officers. The white man had urged his men to kill their officers and had shot dead one officer who mistakenly believed he was a prisoner of the mutineers and tried to rescue him. The renegade was never captured by the British and may have fled into Nepal with other die-hard rebels in the last days of the mutiny.

After six hours, Walpole ordered the Black Watch and Punjabs to retreat back into the jungle. The Black Watch pulled back in parade-ground fashion, file by file. Many resented the order to retreat and believed one final charge would have captured the fort. Walpole refused to authorise another assault and retreated back through the jungle for about two miles to make camp for the night.

During the night, Singh, the renegade and the rest of the defenders abandoned the fort and headed for Bareilly to join the main rebel army; but first they burned their own dead and mutilated and stripped the bodies of the British dead and wounded who lay near the fort.

The attack had cost Walpole's column 100 casualties. The Black Watch lost 41 dead and wounded. Four members of the regiment were awarded the Victoria Cross for recovering dead and wounded while under heavy fire from the stronghold's defenders. Walpole is said to have been so relieved to hear the stronghold's garrison had slipped away that he uttered the words, 'Thank God' when he got the news.

Feelings were running high in the Highland camp against

Walpole. Forbes-Mitchell said it would have only taken one man to attack the general in his tent for many other Highlanders to have joined in. Some spoke of burning the tent with the blundering general inside.

'After we retired from the fort the excitement was so great among the men ... owing to the sacrifice of so many officers and men through sheer mismanagement, that if the officers had given the least encouragement, I am convinced they would have turned out in a body and hanged General Walpole,' he wrote in his memoirs.

Next day the Highland dead were buried as the pipes of the Black Watch and Sutherlands played the 'Flowers of the Forest'. Many of the grizzled Highlanders wept in a mixture of mourning for their fallen comrades and anger at the incompetent Walpole who had sent them to their deaths.

Walpole made sure his artillery pounded the next stronghold he came across with his column before sending in his infantry, but, through his blundering, the garrison managed to escape again. On 27 April he met up with Campbell and the three other British columns for the attack on the rebels at Bareilly. The disaster at Ruiya had encouraged more of the rebels to fight on and probably prolonged the pacification process by several months.

Walpole was awarded a knighthood despite his badly mishandled attack at Ruiya and the contempt he was held in by the soldiers forced to serve under his command. In those days a general almost automatically received a knighthood at the end of a successful campaign.

The reward for all too many of the men who fought and died under Walpole's command was a neglected grave in a jungle far from home.

MOUNTAIN MADNESS

MAJUBA 1881

The veteran soldiers of the Gordon Highlanders should have known better than to taunt their Boer foes from the top of a South African mountain in 1881. The Boer farmers' response to this was to inflict one of the most humiliating defeats the British were to suffer during Queen Victoria's 64-year reign.

The British Empire was at the height of its glory when the Gordons were sent from India to help put down a revolt by Dutch-speaking farmers in the recently annexed Transvaal Republic. The British had taken over the bankrupt republic in 1877 when the Boers felt badly in need of protection from the Zulu warriors of King Cetewayo. But when the British smashed Cetewayo's armies in 1879 and the Transvaal's economy started to improve, the Boers started to hanker for their independence again. Matters reached a head in November 1880 over a minor dispute concerning a wagon tax imposed by the British and soon there were 10,000 armed farmers mustering to fight for the restoration of Transvaal's independence.

The war went badly for the British from the start. A column of British troops heading for the Transvaal was badly cut up by hidden Boer marksmen after its commander rejected a suggestion that he should just turn around and take his men home again. British commanders were soon calling for reinforcements following another bungled attempt to push troops through the passes in the

Drakensberg Mountains, which were the key to a successful invasion of the Transvaal. The British Government had planned to send the Seaforth Highlanders from India to bolster a fresh offensive against the Boers, because the Gordons were due to be returned to Britain; however, the junior officers in the Gordons sent a telegram to the War Office in London begging for a chance to fight in South Africa. The War Office was so impressed by the Gordons' enthusiasm that they were sent instead of the Seaforths.

The Gordons landed in Durban and marched through the port city with bagpipes blaring and kilts swinging. Many of its 700 men had more than 10 years army service behind them and they had earned a reputation as good fighters during their recent service in India. The Highlanders were quick to dismiss the Boers as an undisciplined collection of ragged boys and old greybeards. They had little time for Durban people, who suggested that years spent living on farms and shooting game for the pot meant that many of the Boers were marksmen who knew how to make good use of available cover. All too soon those farmers would be hunting Scotsmen.

The Gordons were sent to join a British force under the command of Major-General Sir George Colley, an officer who was being groomed for stardom by his superiors. Colley was trying to force his way through the Boers that were holding the key mountain pass at Laing's Neck and believed that nearby Majuba Hill was the key to success; if he could capture the hill and outflank the Boer positions, he was sure the farmers would be forced to retreat from the pass. Majuba, an extinct volcano, rose sheer almost 2,000 feet above the surrounding landscape. The Boers believed no British force large enough to threaten them would be able to climb the hill and they did not even bother to post men on it at night.

Colley knew morale in the Boer camp was poor, because promised supplies were not arriving and many of the farmers were anxious to get back to their properties where work was piling up for them to do. He set out from his camp around 10pm on 26 February 1881, with approximately 500 men drawn from the Norfolk Regiment, the Rifle Brigade, the Gordons and a party of sailors. He would be criticised later for cobbling the force together from so many different regiments instead of taking one already cohesive unit, such as the Gordons, with him onto the mountain. Two companies of the Rifle Brigade and one of the three companies of Gordons he had with him were left in support positions along the march route.

The climb up the steep sides of Majuba took some of the soldiers five hours, but others completed it in two. The men were loaded down with 70 rounds of heavy 0.45 ammunition for their single-shot Martini-Henry rifles, three-days'-worth of food, a heavy overcoat, a blanket and a groundsheet. It has been calculated that each soldier was carrying 45 pounds of equipment and some only completed the climb by crawling on all fours.

Colley had approximately 350 men, including 118 Gordons, with him on the top of Majuba. As dawn broke at around 5.45am, some of the Gordons emerged from their positions to taunt the Boers down below. They behaved more like a gang of daytrippers enjoying the morning sunshine than seasoned soldiers.

'Ha ha, got you this time, I think,' and 'Come up you beggars and fight,' were typical of the insults shouted by the Highlanders as they shook their fists at the Boers.

The Boers could not make out what the Gordons, who they dubbed 'Bergskotte', were shouting, but they could see them dancing around the lip of the old volcanic crater in their brown jackets. Colley had at first ordered his men not to fire at the Boers in the hope of keeping the seizure of the summit a secret for as long as possible, but he appears to have changed his mind at some point and one of the officers from the Norfolks borrowed a rifle for a pot shot at the men below.

When the Boers saw the Highlanders capering on the rim of the plateau which capped the mountain, many did believe that they had been outmanoeuvred by Colley and started hitching up their wagons ready for a retreat. But the Boer commander, General Piet Joubert, realised that the British were too far away to hit his men with their rifles and had no long-range artillery on the summit capable of reaching the men defending the pass. He ordered his men to recapture the hill.

A force of 150 of the fittest Boers were chosen for the assault and split into three groups for the climb. The best marksmen in the Boer force were assigned to provide the covering fire that would keep the heads of the British down while the assault teams climbed up Majuba. The Boers were mainly armed with Westley Richards rifles, which were similar to the British Martini-Henrys but more accurate.

Colley had set his men up in a defensive ring around the rim of the plateau with a reserve force sheltered in a dip near the eastern edge. The covering fire provided by the Boer marksmen succeeded in keeping the British behind cover and the assault teams encountered very little fire. The Gordons, on the western edge of the plateau, were the first to feel the sting of the Boers' bullets. While the Boer marksmen fired from a ravine 500 yards further down the hill to keep the Gordons pinned down, small groups of their comrades dashed across a stretch of open ground into cover at the base of the cliffs. The Gordons' commander at this point on the western perimeter, Lieutenant Ian Hamilton, sent a message asking Colley to send him more men, who he planned to use to return the fire coming from the Boer marksmen and shoot down the groups of Boers running across the open ground. Before the reinforcements could arrive, the Boers had sneaked onto a hillock about 70 yards from the Gordons' positions and opened up a devastating fire which killed two or three of the 18 men under Hamilton's command. Colley had earlier refused to give permission to dig trenches, but Hamilton had ordered his men to build up piles of stones in front of their positions to provide some cover behind which to shoot from. This proved a mistake as the heavy 0.45 slugs from the Boer rifles peppered the stones sending shrapnel-like shards all over the place.

The Gordons quickly realised that they had to keep their heads down if they did not want them shot off and after the battle it was noted that nearly all the British dead had been shot at least once in the head; some of the British dead had as many as six bullet wounds. Also, the Gordons' return of fire was far less accurate and it was later discovered that the majority of them had set their rifle sights to shoot at targets 500 yards away.

Colley sent a group of men to help Hamilton but as they moved into position they were suddenly caught in a fusillade of Boer fire which sent 16 of them falling to the ground, dead or wounded. The rest of the reinforcements turned and ran back to Colley's main position.

The Boers had by this time managed to get men on the northern lip of the plateau and Hamilton's men found themselves under fire from two directions. Hamilton ordered his men to follow the reinforcements in their retreat back to the depression where Colley and his reserve troops were sheltering. The Boers shot several of Hamilton's men down as they ran back.

Hamilton urged a bayonet charge to push the Boers back off the summit of the hill, but was refused permission for it. The third Boer assault team was now beginning to come over the eastern lip of the crater near Colley's position. Colley drew the reserves, and the Gordons who had made it to the depression, into a line and ordered them to deliver a volley with their rifles at the advancing Boers. But the farmers flopped to the ground just as the British fired and then jumped up again to shoot at the closely packed line facing them. This was too much for many of the British. Men threw their rifles aside and started to leap from rock to rock down the steep hillside like demented mountain goats; some suffered serious injuries when they plunged over the 30-foot cliffs which ringed much of the plateau's edge.

Colley, still wearing the carpet slippers he had put on for the climb up Majuba, was shot through the head and died. His admirers would later claim he was killed while trying to rally his troops. His detractors, and this included several of the Gordons' officers, said Colley was trying to surrender. By 1pm the only British left on the hill were dead, dying or prisoners.

Hamilton was among the men captured on the hill. He had

been standing near Colley when he saw the barrel of a Boer rifle pointing in his direction. The Boer was quicker on the trigger than Hamilton and the Scot's wrist had been shattered by a bullet. Hamilton then decided to join the general retreat but as he reached the edge of the plateau, a ricocheting bullet or a rock splinter hit him the back of the head and knocked him out. He awoke to find a Boer standing over him and fingering the broadsword his father, a former colonel of the Gordons, had given him. It was to be 20 years and another war against the Boers before the sword was returned.

Another Gordons' officer also lost his sword when it was taken as a trophy by the Boers. Lieutenant Hector Macdonald had risen through the ranks from private and had only recently been made an officer. He was in command of 20 men stationed on a small hill at the southern edge of the crater. One-by-one his men were killed or wounded by the Boer marksmen until only he and a lance corporal were left unwounded. Even then, Macdonald was determined to fight to the last and he was reduced to throwing rocks at the Boers as they finally closed in around him. Macdonald surrendered, but his temper flared when a young Boer tried to grab his sporran. He kicked the boy in the stomach and was lucky to escape being shot dead in retaliation. Sporrans and kilts were poplar trophies among the Boers and many of the Gordons killed on the hill were stripped. The kilts were given to Boer women for dress material while the sporrans were proudly displayed by hanging them from the mantels over fireplaces in farm parlours.

Macdonald was given his sword back by General Joubert, who had been impressed by his bravery. He and some of his fellow Gordons mounted a ceremonial guard over Colley's body the night after the battle. Macdonald ended his career as a general, but his end was sad; 'Fighting Mac' blew his brains out in a Paris hotel room in 1903 en route from Ceylon to answer charges of homosexuality.

Hamilton also rose to be a general and lived until 1947. But his reputation was tarnished beyond redemption by his handling of the First World War's disastrous Gallipoli Campaign in 1915.

The disaster at Majuba led the British Liberal Government to make a quick peace with the Boers and the Transvaal was soon an independent republic again. The British Army ordered an inquiry, but not surprisingly found that everyone involved blamed someone else for the tragedy.

The Gordons' officers were proud of their huntin', shootin' and fishin' gentlemen-of-leisure image and the fact that none of them had ever attended staff college, but even they realised some lessons would have to be learned from the disaster. The regiment held its own inquiry.

While the officers had their say at the various official inquiries, the ordinary soldiers let their fists do the talking whenever the battle was mentioned. The Norfolks blamed the Gordons for the disaster, the Rifle Brigade maintained if they had been holding the plateau, there would have been no defeat and all the soldiers agreed that the sailors at Majuba had let everyone else down.

About the only people who did not play the blame game were the dead Gordons lying lined up, pale and nearly naked, in a row on the top of Majuba Hill, their glazed eyes staring blindly from bloodied heads at the African sky.

The Gordons had suffered 45 dead and 52 wounded out of the British total of 92 killed and 134 wounded and 59 captured. In contrast, the Boers had one fatality and five wounded, one of whom would die later.

Those early morning taunts shouted at the Boers had cost the Gordons dear.

HIGHLAND HUMILIATION

MAGERSFONTEIN 1899

Now forgotten by a nation proud of its military heritage, the Battle of Magersfontein during the Great Boer War plunged Scotland into national mourning shortly before Christmas 1899. Not only was the fabled Highland Brigade routed, but many of its men fled the battle like frightened rabbits.

What went wrong?

The Brigade was made up by battalions of four of the most famous regiments in the British Army – The Black Watch, the Seaforth Highlanders, the Highland Light Infantry (HLI) and the Argyll and Sutherland Highlanders. Since the 1740s the Highland Regiments had been regarded in British military circles as stormtroopers, far better when used in attack than in defence. The Black Watch was the oldest and most prestigious of the Highland Regiments; it first paraded as a regular infantry battalion in May 1740 and had since fought on four continents.

The Argyll and Sutherland Highlanders' second battalion had been immortalised during the Crimean War in 1855 by *The Times* war correspondent William Russell as the 'thin red streak' which would later become known as the immortal 'Thin Red Line'.

The Seaforths arrived in South Africa with a good reputation earned on the North-West Frontier in India. The regiment still recruited heavily in the Highlands, and its men were reputed to be strapping examples of manhood with a healthy taste for whisky. The

Highland Light Infantry were the only soldiers in the brigade who were clad in trousers instead of kilts. The other Highland regiments looked down on them as the sweepings of Glasgow's slums; however, only four other regiments in the British Army had more battle honours.

The Black Watch were also men with something to prove. In 1884 the 'Fuzzy-Wuzzies' had broken into a British square during the Sudan Campaign and the Black Watch was blamed for the incident. For years afterwards, members of other regiments would start fights in bars frequented by men from the Black Watch by loudly ordering a pint of 'Broken Square'.

When the Highland Brigade marched into Lieutenant-General Lord Methuen's camp in December 1899 with their kilts swinging and pipes skirling, there were high hopes that they would work their old storming magic on the enemy Boer farmers entrenched somewhere up ahead on the road to the besieged mining town of Kimberley.

Methuen had already made three failed attempts to reach Kimberley. On each occasion the Boers had inflicted heavy casualties on the British before retreating to their next line of defences in the hills. Methuen did not impress the men of the Highland Brigade. Captain Archibald Cameron of the Black Watch was amongst those who voiced concern about Methuen as a military commander.

'I do not consider the morale of this camp is good,' he wrote. 'Everyone has entirely lost confidence in Methuen. He just banged his head against Belmont and Grasfan without any previous artillery preparation, and Modder River was disgraceful.'*

Methuen's latest plan was once again for a head-on attack on the Boer positions. The attack was to be preceded by the heaviest bombardment fired by the Royal Artillery since the Crimean War more than 40 years before. There was only one problem – the Boers were not where the British thought they were.

* The Battle of Modder River on 28 November 1899 was another military disappointment for the British forces in South Africa and Methuen was in command.

In previous battles the Boers had always dug their trenches along the crests of the hills they were defending. The Boer positions at Magersfontein were dominated by the Magersfontein ridge itself and that was where the British artillery believed the Boers would be. But Boer leader General Koos de la Rey had realised it was better to put the trenches at the foot of the ridge. Shooting down from the crest would leave an area at the very base of the ridge which the rifle shot could not reach. De la Rey also wanted to keep his men further away from their ponies. In past encounters with the British his men had been too quick to fire off a few rounds then mount up and retreat.

Methuen delayed his advance for two weeks and that gave the Boers time to dig a strong trench system at Magersfontein. A lack of reconnaissance meant that the British were unaware of the trenches until their soldiers literally stumbled into them. Methuen thought that too much reconnaissance would tip the Boers off that an attack was coming. A balloon which would have spotted the Boer trenches arrived the day before the Highland Brigade attack, but was not used.

Methuen's plan was to use the Highland Brigade to storm the Magersfontein ridge at dawn on 11 December 1899. The Guards Brigade and the 12th Lancers were to protect their right flank while the King's Own Yorkshire Light Infantry and the 9th Lancers occupied the ground on the far right of the British position. Methuen planned to send the Northumberland Fusiliers and the Northamptonshire Regiment to protect the Highlanders' left flank.

Everything depended on the Highland Brigade and its Major-General Andy Wauchope. Wauchope, known to his adoring men and the Scottish public as General Andy, was one of the richest men in Scotland thanks to his ownership of several highly productive coal mines. He had been wounded several times in his 34-year military career.

Wauchope was far from keen on trying to navigate the boulder and scrub-strewn South African veldt in the pitch dark of a moonless night with 4,000 men. However, when his officers urged him to ask Methuen to rethink the plan, he refused. He did, however, strike a note of gloom when he spoke to the commander of the Guards Brigade, who felt cheated that the Highlanders looked set to grab all the glory. 'Things don't go always as they are expected,' he told his colleague as they left Methuen's briefing together. 'You may not be in reserve for long.'

The heavy artillery bombardment proved to be a waste of time. The tonnes of high explosive lobbed at the Boers resulted in only three wounded and one piece of valuable information revealed by the action went ignored. A Black Watch sergeant noticed that the shells that fell short of the ridge threw up a different colour of dirt than the rest. 'There must be trenches there,' he observed. But in those days officers could still go through their whole career without speaking to an ordinary soldier and the sergeant's suspicions went unreported at the time.

The Highlanders spent the night before the attack camped about three miles from Magersfontein. It rained heavily and the South African night chilled them to the bone, but the men were forbidden to light any fires; many of them had last eaten at midday.

Shortly after midnight, as the moon finally set, the brigade began its advance in the densest formation of the British Army drill book – the quarter column. This packed the men into 90 lines of 45 men each across a 45-yard frontage.

The Black Watch were in the lead, the men on far left holding a guide line; then came the Seaforths, followed by the Argylls and Sutherlands and finally the HLI. Many of the Highlanders clung to the kilt of the man ahead of them as they plodded through the inky black darkness of the moonless night.

'We stumbled over rocks and dykes, and I fancy the regiments behind were in a fearful muddle as some of the Seaforths got mixed in with my company,' recalled the Black Watch's captain, CE Stewart. 'We kept tacking about in the most extraordinary way until we came to a line of bushes with only one place through.'

The guide leading the brigade was Major GE Benson of the Royal Artillery, later one of the top anti-guerrilla column commanders in the British Army. He carried two compasses, but the iron stone boulders that littered the veldt sent their needles spinning in crazy directions. Lightning flashed and thunder boomed as the column stumbled blindly towards disaster.

Shortly before 4am, the tightly packed ranks of the lead company arrived about 500 yards from Magersfontein and Benson urged Wauchope to begin spreading the troops out into their attack formations. 'This is as far as it is safe to go in mass,' he told the general, but Wauchope, marching at the head of the column with his trusty claymore in his hand, wanted to move forward slightly. 'I'm afraid the men will lose direction,' he said. 'I think we will go a little further.'

As dawn was breaking and the lead lines of the Black Watch began to spread out into their assault positions, all hell broke loose.

'It was as if someone had switched on a million electric lights,' said one sergeant. The Boer bullets whizzed high over the heads of the Black Watch and ripped into the packed ranks behind them.

'You can't possibly imagine the number of bullets that came whistling over us,' Lieutenant Archie Bulloch of the Black Watch later wrote. 'Talk of hail stones: that would have been a trifle to us.'

The sudden fusillade caused panic. Officers began shouting contradictory orders. Some men turned on their heels and ran while others tried to move into their attack formations. None of the men and few of the officers knew or understood Wauchope's plan.

'This is fighting, AG!' Wauchope announced to his cousin, Lieutenant AG Wauchope, as he organised the deployment of the Black Watch, with the Boer bullets zipping past him. Minutes later he and the Black Watch's commanding officer, Lieutenant-Colonel John Coode, were shot dead and Lieutenant Wauchope was severely wounded.

'What a pity,' breathed the general as he fell to the ground.

Behind him the men who ran away after the initial volley were rallied by their officers and the Argylls' Pipe-Major James MacKay, who struck up the 'The Campbells are Coming'. The commander of the HLI had been trampled to the ground in the initial rush.

More officers rallied the wandering groups of Highlanders and sent them forward again.

'The result was that men would collect [in groups of] between 50 and 100 and walk towards the trenches again, all separately and with no plan, no object till the men would go no further and run away ... and the poor devils cannot be altogether blamed,' recounted Lieutenant Roger Poore. 'It only shows that a little lack of foresight can demoralise one of the finest bodies of men ... Even so, if a little generalship had been used and a second organised attack made, I believe a second organised attack would have carried the position.'

However, all was not yet lost; some Highlanders began creeping towards the Boer trenches. Around 200 men from the Seaforths and the Black Watch found a weakly held part of the Boer defence line and were pushing into it when they were mistakenly shelled by the British artillery. A 70-strong force of Scandinavian volunteers fighting for the Boers was overrun after the British shells landed on their position, killing most of them. A party of Seaforths almost broke through when they stumbled on a gap in the Boer defences and they would have broken clean through if they hadn't encountered the Boer General Piet Cronje, who managed to pin them down with rifle fire until reinforcements could arrive.

Poor communications meant that none of the British successes were reinforced until it was too late. The deputy brigade commander, Lieutenant-Colonel James Hughes-Hallet of the Seaforths, did not even know Wauchope was dead until several hours later.

The British artillery by now had both the Highlanders and Boers pinned down in their positions. Two companies of Seaforths had been left behind during the night march and they now advanced in short bounds to within 50 yards of the Boer trenches.

'In a few minutes the bullets began to "whizz" around us so thickly that we had to lie down and take as much cover behind bushes as we could,' recalled Private Fred Bly of the Seaforths. 'About eight o'clock we were within 250 yards of the enemy's trenches and we were stuck for hours as our artillery were firing over our heads and dropping the shells just in front of us.'

By 6am the Highland attack was completely stalled. Boer marksmen picked off any man who tried to move. Highlanders lay behind folds in the ground or anthills as the blazing sun burned into the backs of their naked knees. Many men dozed off in the stifling South African heat as clouds of flies buzzed around them. Only the occasional rifle shot and the low moans of the wounded disturbed the quiet.

'About ten am I could find only three sound men within thirty yards of each side,' wrote Captain Stewart. 'We hugged the ground pretty close after we had finished our rounds.'

Although each man had been issued with 150 rounds of ammunition before the attack, many of them were running short. One enterprising officer from the Argylls, Lieutenant Bertrand Lang, avoided having the backs of his knees roasted in the sun as he was wearing a pair of women's black woollen stockings. He most likely bought them to protect his legs from the thorny bushes he expected to encounter on the night march.

The Guards Brigade had already been moving into its position on the right of the Highlanders when the dawn broke and the Boers opened fire. Almost immediately, Highlanders started to appear in front of the Guards' ranks.

'I was in the firing line, we advanced in extended order, meeting these wretched Highlanders, quite disorganised, in twos and threes, without helmets or rifles,' recalled Lieutenant Harry Pryce-Jones of the Coldstream Guards.

Around mid-morning Methuen tried to break the stalemate by sending his only reserve troops, the Gordon Highlanders, into the attack. The Gordons were fresh from India, where they had gained fame for storming a heavily defended enemy position on the Heights of Tirah on the North-West Frontier.

They moved forward at about 11am in military text book 'fire and movement' leapfrogs. But then they came up against a barbed wire boundary fence which they could not cut and their advance ground to a halt. Disaster then struck around 1.30pm. Hughes-Hallet spotted a large party of Boers threatening to outflank the Highland Brigade from the right and ordered some of his men to swing around to face the new threat. However, the tired and frustrated Highlanders mistook the re-deployment for a general retreat. Hundreds rose to their feet and began heading back towards the British camp. The Boers poured bullets into the backs of the retreating Highlanders.

'This was disastrous, for as we exposed ourselves the Boers dropped our fellows in dozens,' recalled Private Bly. The retreat quickly turned into a foot race.

'Then I saw a sight that I hope never to see again: the men of the Highland Brigade running for all they were worth, others cowering under bushes, behind guns, some lying under their blankets, officers running about threatening to shoot them, urging on some, kicking others,' wrote Lieutenant Poore. Captain WL Foster of the Royal Artillery also witnessed the retreat.

'As they came streaming back to our guns, they were no longer men, they had no nerves, did not know where they were,' he recalled.

Some water wagons were waiting for the Highlanders and as they thirstily gathered around them the previously silent Boer artillery guns opened fire. A volley of shells sent the Highlanders running again and this time there was no rallying them. There were still large numbers of Highlanders lying out in front of the Boer trenches.

The Black Watch's Captain Stewart fell asleep in the sun at around 3pm. About three hours later, after the last of the men around him had run out ammunition, the Boers came out of their trenches with canteens of water for the Highlanders. The Boers even offered to let the Scots walk away unmolested if they would leave their rifles behind. Stewart refused the offer.

After darkness fell on the battlefield, the last of the diehards filtered back to the British lines. Almost 1,000 of Methuen's men were dead or wounded; the Highland Brigade had lost about 750 men, the Black Watch lost 60% of its officers and the commanding officers of the Black Watch, Argylls and Gordons were all dead.

The Boers lost 250 men from a defending force of around 6,500. Methuen's attacking force totalled nearer 15,000. After the battle, members of every battalion accused men from the other regiments of leading the charge to the rear.

In amongst the chaos, bravery and cowardice, one of the HLI's medics managed to earn himself a Victoria Cross for bravery. Corporal John Shaul, an Englishman whose father was a sergeant in the Royal Scots, was one of the HLI's stretcher bearers and was seen braving the Boer's bullets several times to treat wounded comrades lying out on the open veldt. Shaul, 26-years-old at the time, had joined the regiment 11 years earlier and was later to rise to the rank of band sergeant before leaving the army in 1910 to work at a South African mine.

The defeat plunged Scotland into national mourning. The popular press had turned the Highland regiments and their commanders into national icons. As far as the public was concerned the 'kilties' had never lost a battle fought in Queen Victoria's name.

The Highland Brigade's losses were replaced and it was placed under the command of another Highland hero, Major-General Hector 'Fighting Mac' Macdonald. Unlike Wauchope and most present-day British generals, Macdonald had risen to command from the ranks. The brigade fought well for the remainder of the Boer war, which dragged on until 1902, but never again were its men thought of as the stormtroopers of the British Empire.

Wauchope and his men were portrayed in the press as lambs sent to the slaughter by Methuen. Contemporary newspaper reports spoke of men hung up on a maze of barbed wire fences cunningly positioned by the Boers in front of their trenches. In reality no barbed wire entanglements had been laid out. There was only a farm fence and the fence marking the boundary between the British-ruled Cape Colony and the Orange Free State.

Methuen, in a misguided attempt to soothe Scottish outrage by praising the Highland Brigade, stoked popular ire when he said,

'We were within an ace of carrying the position … everything depended on one word. That word was "Forward!" '

In fact, Methuen had put his finger on one of the main reasons the attack failed – lack of communication on the battlefield. The same problem would dog the British 15 years later during the First World War when breakthroughs would go unexploited because the generals were unaware they had taken place until it was too late. Many of the fresh generation of Gordons, Seaforths and Argylls who fought in the First World War found themselves surrounded and annihilated after breaking through the German lines and then finding themselves cut off.

On a poignant note, the level of casualties which had sent Scotland into the depths of despair in 1899 went almost unnoticed or unreported in the First World War.

IN DUBLIN'S FAIR CITY

BACHELOR'S WALK 1914

At the outbreak of the First World War in August 1914, while other units from the British garrison in Dublin marched through the city to rousing cheers from the population, one battalion was greeted with hoots and spat at. The King's Own Scottish Borderers had earned the hatred of Dubliners only a week earlier when it had killed three people and wounded scores more by opening fire on an angry mob.

The mob had gathered to protest against the double standard displayed by the British army when it came to dealing with gunrunning. Ireland was on the brink of civil war over plans to grant the country semi-independent status, popularly referred to as Home Rule. The mainly Protestant population in the north-east of the country had begun to arm itself to resist the Home Rule plan claiming that for the mainly Catholic island it would in reality be Rome Rule from the Vatican.

Thousands of rifles were smuggled into the Ireland by the Unionists under the noses of the British authorities in Ireland; by March 1914, the situation was regarded as so serious by the British authorities that it was decided to make preparations to send the British army into the northern counties to guarantee the rule of law, but the British Army at that time had a high number of Irish Protestant officers. When the troops stationed at the Curragh army base near Dublin heard that they might be sent north, the commander of the 3rd Cavalry Brigade, Irishman Hubert Gough, and 57 of his officers announced that they would rather resign than go.

The officers of the King's Own Scottish Borderers were also caught up in the row. At first all but the commanding officer, his deputy and one other officer voted to quit the army rather than serve against the Protestants in the north. As the deadline for a final decision to be made approached, most of the officers reconsidered their position and agreed to obey whatever orders they were given. However, 10 held out and promised to resign.

The British authorities caved in and gave assurances that no officer would be sent north against his will and, as it turned out, the army was not used against the Protestants. The cave-in did not improve the Nationalist majority in Ireland's faith in British goodwill and even-handedness.

British claims to impartiality took another blow in the eyes of the Nationalists a month later in April 1914 when the Unionist Ulster Volunteer Force landed 35,000 rifles and five million rounds of ammunition at the northern port of Larne without any official interference. The password used by the smugglers, if such a blatant arms landing can be called smuggling, was 'Gough'.

In the eyes of the Nationalists, what was good for the goose should also be good for the gander and it was decided to import a consignment of German rifles. On 26 July the yacht *Asgard* arrived at the seaside town of Howth, about eight miles east of Dublin, with a cargo of 900 rifles and 29,000 rounds of ammunition. The yacht was captained by the spy novelist Erskine Childers.

Around 800 members of the Irish Volunteers, the Nationalists' answer to the Ulster Volunteer Force, turned up to protect the landing and help move the rifles to Dublin. Many of the men carried clubs and a few were armed with revolvers. They blocked the roads into Howth while the guns and ammunition were unloaded. It was at this point that the King's Own Scottish Borderers entered the story.

They were called in by the Dublin Metropolitan Police to help block the main road from Howth to Dublin. The police had feared the Nationalists' new rifles would be turned on them if they interfered with the landing. In fact, the ammunition was sent to Dublin by another route and the rifles were not be loaded. The 160 King's Own Scottish Borderers sent to help the police were put on trams which took them to the eastern outskirts of Dublin. A later government inquiry determined that the soldiers should never have been called out because there was no risk of public disorder and the arms smuggling was a matter for the customs service to deal with.

The crowd accompanying the handcarts transporting the arms was confronted near Kilbarrack by a line of soldiers standing with bayonets fixed to their rifles. There was a scuffle as the crowd tried to brush the British cordon aside and one or two people received slight cuts from the bayonets. A revolver was fired and the bullet grazed two of the soldiers. However, the confrontation quickly turned to apparent negotiation. While the men at the front of the procession kept the British talking, their colleagues slipped out of the column with most of the rifles. In all, the soldiers and police officers only managed to confiscate 20 rifles.

The troops then set off to march back to Dublin. As they marched, more and more people joined the crowd jeering at them and throwing the occasional stone. By the time the soldiers reached Bachelor's Walk in Dublin, the mob was big enough to bring the soldiers to a halt.

What happened next is unclear. The only thing that is certain is that the soldiers started firing into the crowd. One version has it that a British officer raised his hand to quiet the crowd and the soldiers mistook this for a signal to open fire. The Royal Inquiry held later into the incident concluded that the 21 soldiers who fired into the crowd believed they were acting on orders.

Most versions of events that day say that three people were killed, but others put the death toll at four. All agree that at least one of the people killed had nothing to do with the angry mob that was confronting the troops. The Nationalist propaganda machine quickly swung into action and portrayed the shooting as a cold-blooded slaughter of innocents. Much was made of the difference between the way the arms landing at Howth was treated compared to the one at Larne.

The outbreak of the First World War a week later resulted in a surge of pro-war sentiment in working-class Dublin. The Dublin population gave the various British Army units rousing cheers as they marched to the docks on their way to France to fight the Germans. All but the King's Own Scottish Borderers.

Two years later, the rifles landed at Howth were put to use against the British garrison in Dublin when the Nationalists seized key buildings in the city and proclaimed an Irish republic. The rebels were defeated and imprisoned. However, when some of the ringleaders were executed by firing squad, public opinion turned against the British.

The end of the First World War in 1918 saw the election of a majority of republican MPs who refused to recognise the British Government in Westminster. A vicious guerrilla war broke out which resulted in Ireland being divided into two self-governing parts in 1922. Most counties in Ireland became part of the Irish Free State but the six in the north-east retained closer links to Britain as Northern Ireland.

The deaths on Bachelor's Walk helped stoke the fires of Nationalist resentment and the echoes of those shots fired that day in July 1914 sounded for many years afterwards.

INFIRMARY BLUES

BEDFORD 1914

German machine-guns and barbed wire were not the only hazards that the 51st Highland Division faced during the First World War. Childhood diseases took a heavy toll of the young men of the division when they moved from Scotland to the Bedford area of southern England for training before being sent over to France. Many of the soldiers were from remote glens and islands where they had never been exposed to the childhood diseases such as mumps, chickenpox and measles which were rife in more populated areas of Britain. Hundreds of the young Scottish soldiers were hospitalised and 85 died from the diseases and their complications before the division was sent overseas.

But the time spent around Bedford was not all misery; there were some laughs as well. The arrival of the Highlanders led to rumours sweeping the Bedford area that Britain's ally Russia had sent troops to England. Some people even said the Russians still had snow on their boots. It turned out that people had been seen Gaelic-speaking members of the 4th Seaforth Highlanders arriving in the area and encountered a language barrier. The battalion came not from Russia, but from Ross-shire.

Curiously enough, the arrival in the south of England of the 2nd Battalion of the Ross-shire Highlanders 190 years before had also played havoc with their health. The battalion was formed of around 600 boys recruited from the estates of Lord Seaforth. When the boys arrived in Kent in 1805, their health rapidly deteriorated. The youngsters went down with a variety of skin diseases, swellings and tumours.

The cause of the problems was eventually found to be a change in the youngsters' diet. They had been brought up on barley and oatmeal and the army rations given to them contained more meat than their digestive systems could cope with. Once the boys got used to the army food, their health improved.

A SIGNAL DISASTER

GRETNA 1915

The men of the 7th Royal Scots thought that they were heading off to war – instead they were heading for the worst train wreck in British history. The battalion was a Territorial Army unit based in Leith and when the First World War was declared in August 1914, the men volunteered for service overseas. However, instead of going to France, they spent the first winter of the war guarding the shore defences along the Firth of Forth near their homes.

Finally, it was decided to send them as reinforcements to the beleaguered British troops involved in the futile battles to capture the Gallipoli peninsula in Turkey. The peninsula commanded the narrow neck of water which linked the Mediterranean to the Sea of Marmara and the Turkish capital of Istanbul. The British High Command hoped that if they could capture Gallipoli they would be able to send a fleet through the straits which would then blast Istanbul until the Turks renounced their alliance with Germany.

The 7th Royal Scots were to be sent on two trains from Larbert, near Stirling, to Liverpool, where a troopship was waiting to take them to the Mediterranean. Around 470 men from A and D Companies were loaded on the first of the two trains, which was due to leave Larbert in the early hours of 22 May 22 1915.

The musicians of the battalion's pipe band were loaded into the train's first carriage. The signallers were packed the second carriage. The third carriage, which was First Class, was reserved for the officers and the rest of the two companies were distributed in the carriages behind. For some reason, it was decided to lock the men in their carriage compartments.

The soldiers soon began to doze or play cards as the carriages rocked their way south through the night and into the early hours of the next morning. None had any notion as the train gathered speed down the incline which led to the last signal box in Scotland of the disaster waiting to happen just ahead of them. There was a train sitting parked on the southbound line outside the signal box at Quintinshill Junction near Gretna.

The slow-moving local train from Carlisle had been moved off the northbound line to make way for the express from Euston, which was running 45 minutes late. In normal circumstances, the local train would have been switched onto a siding until the express passed through, but that night there were two goods trains already occupying the sidings. The signalmen in the box at Quintinshill had been switching shifts and despite the fact that the newly arrived man, James Tinsley, had just got off the local train from Carlisle, he signalled the troop train through.

By the time the troop-train driver saw the stationary train on the southbound line ahead of him, it was too late to stop. The troop train careered into the Carlisle train at about 70 miles per hour. The force compacted the troop train to about half its length and piled the front carriages up into a twisted mass of wood and metal 30 feet high. Matters soon got very much worse. As men staggered from the wreckage onto the northbound line, the Euston express train ploughed into them and hot coals spilling from the boiler furnaces of the two engines pulling the express then set fire to the gas escaping from the cylinders which fed the lights on the troop train.

Soldiers trapped in the wreckage begged their comrades to shoot them as the fire spread and began consuming them; some trapped men hacked at their own arms and legs with knives and bayonets in a bid to free themselves. Seeing the fire threatening to engulf the whole troop train, some of the surviving soldiers unhooked the car carrying the ammunition from the rear and pushed it down the track away from the inferno. A local fire engine was quickly on the scene and helped stop the fire from spreading by spraying down the carriages still untouched by the blaze.

An ambulance train was sent from Carlisle in response to the disaster. The doctors who arrived on it were soon amputating limbs on site to free the trapped survivors of the crash as the firemen continued to play their hoses on the wreckage in a bid to keep the flames back. When the soldiers were mustered for a roll-call near the crash scene, only 57 answered their names. The crash had cost the battalion 211 dead and 246 injured. Civilian casualties were far lighter – only 16 of them were killed.

The battalion's injured were sent back to Leith, but the men who answered the roll-call found themselves put on another train to continue their journey to Liverpool. It was not until their troopship, the *Empress of Britain*, was about to sail for the Mediterranean that it was decided to put the crash survivors back on shore. Looking bedraggled and without much of their equipment, the men were mistaken for prisoners of war by Liverpool children who stoned them.

Tinsley, the man who signalled the troop train through, was sentenced to three years hard labour for his part in the tragedy. His colleague George Meakin was jailed for 18 months. The soldiers of the Royal Scots had been prepared to die for king and country in battle overseas, and many of the battalion who did reach Gallipoli did just that. None had expected to die before they had even left Scotland.

BLOODING THE PUPS

GULLY RAVINE 1915

After the Turkish machine-gun fire had finished scything the young
Scots soldiers of the 8th Scottish Rifles down, a brush fire began to
creep across the battlefield to incinerate the wounded where they
lay. For the majority of the Glasgow men, the Battle of Gully Ravine
in 1915 was their first and last taste of battle. The battle was one of
many that year as the British tried to capture the Gallipoli peninsula
in a campaign they believed would knock Turkey out the First
World War. The campaign is rated as one of Britain's worst military
cock-ups.

Inadequate equipment coupled with inadequate leadership led
to a major defeat and the deaths of 37,000 British Empire troops.
Gallipoli has become an icon for Australians and New Zealanders
who bleat to this day about the callous British sacrifice of the cream
of antipodean manhood, but of those 37,000 men who fell, 25,000
were British soldiers; the British generals were just, if not more,
careless about the loss of their own countrymen's lives.

Among the lives thrown away were those of the young
volunteer soldiers of the Glasgow-based 8th Scottish Rifles. The
battalion was composed of 'weekend warriors' of the Territorial
Army who had volunteered en masse for service overseas when the
First World War broke out in August 1914. The Territorial Army was
intended for home defence and its part-time soldiers could not be
forced to serve outside Britain.

The eager young Scots landed in Gallipoli in mid-June 1915 to join a campaign which had been going wrong almost from the start. The seizure of the peninsula was the brainchild of Winston Churchill, who was First Lord of the Admiralty at the time. The thin neck of land controlled the narrows which led from the Mediterranean into the Sea of Marmara and ultimately to the Turkish capital of Istanbul. Churchill believed that if British warships could get through the Dardanelles straits into the Sea of Marmara and shell Istanbul, then the Turks would surrender and Germany would have lost one of its most important allies.

When the naval expedition was first mooted, the straits were only defended by a few ancient coastal guns and some minefields. The Royal Navy tried to sail through the narrows with a fleet of second-rate battleships and fishing boats converted to minesweepers. However, the attempt was a fiasco. The Turks responded by sending more troops and artillery guns to Gallipoli.

After the failure of the purely Royal Navy attempt to force the narrows, it was agreed that the Gallipoli peninsula would have to be captured and British artillery stationed there to silence the Turkish big guns which were preventing the minesweepers from doing their job. The decision to send soldiers to Gallipoli was not popular with British Army commanders. The senior generals believed that the war could only be won by defeating the Germans in France and Belgium and any other campaign was an unwelcome diversion of manpower and equipment.

Throughout the campaign the troops at Gallipoli were hampered by a lack of artillery. The sun-parched peninsula was made of a series of knife-edged ridges and hills intersected with steep ravines and gullies. It was perfect country for defence and the only way to pry the Turks out of their well-constructed trenches was with high explosive shells fired from modern artillery guns. But at least one of the British artillery pieces sent to Gallipoli was taken out of a museum and most of the others had first seen action in 1898 in the Sudanese desert. All the modern guns being built in British factories were being sent directly to the Western Front.

The troops sent to fight in Gallipoli were no luckier when it came to their generals; they were also the men the British Army felt it could spare from the 'real war' in France and Belgium. Top of the list of bad generals was the invasion force commander, Scottish General Sir Ian Hamilton. He had no experience of the type of trench warfare being fought on the peninsula and believed that the cold steel of the British bayonet was still the real key to victory. He looked on his Turkish opponents as dirty and stupid.

'They have always been good at trench work where their stupid men have only simple straightforward duties to perform, namely in sticking on and shooting anything that comes up to them,' he was to write in the diary he kept during the campaign and later published.

But Hamilton's biggest problem was that he refused to act as a commander. He believed it was his job to come up with an overall plan and then leave the details of its execution to his subordinates. He made suggestions to his commanders rather than ordering them to do things. Avoiding hurting his subordinates' feelings by correcting their gross errors appears to have taken priority over saving the lives of his soldiers. The 62-year-old's grip on the battles being fought by his men was further hampered by his decision to direct the campaign almost entirely from the offshore island of Imbros, or from ships anchored off the peninsula. No general in Gallipoli needed more supervision than fellow Scot, Lieutenant-General Aylmer Hunter-Weston. The British generals on the peninsula were a sorry bunch to begin with, but Hunter-Weston was surely their Clown Prince.

Hunter-Weston had commanded the first big British landings at the southern tip of the peninsula. Although heavy opposition was met at two of the landing beaches, many of Hunter-Weston's men went ashore on the other beaches almost unopposed. Their priority should have been to move off the beaches and capture the high ground which dominated them. Instead, the troops, lacking orders from Hunter-Weston, sat on the beaches and brewed tea. By the time they did start advancing again, Turkish reinforcements had arrived and were entrenching themselves on the high ground. The next few weeks saw Hunter-Weston's men launch a series of futile and costly attacks on that high ground.

Hunter-Weston rejoiced in the nickname Hunter Bunter, a reference to the popular children's magazine character Billy Bunter. But behind the jovial nickname was a callous, vain, bombastic and unimaginative man; he once gave a bravery medal to an officer for shooting three of his own men during a battle.

'Casualties, what do I care for casualties,' was his often-heard mantra. While casualties in the short term have to be accepted to save lives in the long term, the slaughters Hunter-Weston organised during his career were often the result of sheer stupidity. It was into Hunter-Weston's command that the 8th Scottish Rifles and the other three battalions of the 52nd Lowland Division's 156th Infantry Brigade were placed.

The brigade was the first part of the division to go ashore. The sheer weight of manpower being thrown into the meat-grinder of trench warfare on the peninsula was expected to make up for the lack of modern effective artillery. Gallipoli and the war on the Western Front were both fought on the principle of attrition. The British generals believed that if their troops could kill one enemy soldier for every one of them who died, then the enemy would run out of men first and the war would be won. The entry of the United States into the war on the side of the French and British in 1917 guaranteed victory on the Western Front. However, attrition warfare did not work in Gallipoli; the Turks lost an estimated 350,000 dead and wounded compared with the Western Allies' 170,000 dead, wounded and sick, but still won.

The British evacuation from Gallipoli, after Hamilton was replaced, is still taught to army officers as a classic example of how a withdrawal should be managed. It was the only thing the British did right during that whole ill-fated venture.

The 156th Brigade, all Territorial Army men, had no idea what they had got themselves into. The patriotic and probably naive young men from the working-class streets of Glasgow, Leith and

Edinburgh, had little notion of what attrition warfare was. It was certainly nothing like the tales of the Empire 'do-or-die' that they had been raised on.

From the minute they landed, the Scots were within range of the Turkish artillery guns further inland. This forced the men to live in coffin-shaped holes hacked out of the sun-hardened earth. The water they were issued was so heavily chlorinated that it was almost undrinkable and the massive swarms of flies made for an unwelcome dietary supplement with every spoonful of food they put in their mouths.

The men had only been in Gallipoli a week or so when Hunter-Weston decided to throw the brigade into action on 28 June alongside the veteran troops of the 29th Division, who had been involved in the initial invasion landings.

The brigade and the 29th Division were to launch an attack on the far west side of the peninsula, where a dried up stream bed ran at right angles to the Turkish trenches; the stream bed was known to the British as Gully Ravine and to the Turks as Zighin Dere. The troops from the 29th Division were to storm the trenches on the western, coastal side of the ravine and the key Boomerang Redoubt on its eastern lip. The men of 156th Brigade were to capture two lines of trenches running east from Boomerang Redoubt. The further east the trenches ran, the less cover was available to the advancing British troops. The 8th Scottish Rifles were assigned the trenches furthest east. The first trench line was marked on British military maps as H12.

It was decided that the 29th Division would get priority when it came to the meagre artillery support available to support the attack. What the Scots did not realise was that that translated into virtually no artillery support for them at all.

High explosive shells are needed to deal with trenches, but what the Scots got were a few shrapnel shells which sent some metal fragments raining down on the heads of the Turks who were foolish enough not to take cover. All the British artillery fire did for the Scots was let the Turks know an attack was coming. The Turks responded by shelling the Scots trenches which were packed with men getting ready for the attack. The 8th Scottish Rifles suffered so many casualties from the Turkish shelling that the 7th Scottish Rifles in reserve had to send up 30 men to act as replacements before the attack had even begun.

Zero hour was 11am and right on schedule the officers of the 8th Scottish Rifles led their men clambering out of their trenches for the advance across No Man's Land. It was a massacre. The machine-guns in the Turkish trenches chattered away steadily as they moved from left to right and back again, mowing down the advancing Scots. But it was to get even worse than that. The Turks had a previously undetected machine-gun set up in a position where it could fire from the east along the lines of advancing Scottish soldiers. It was a machine-gunner's dream because the target was 50 to 60 men deep.

The Scots fell in bunches and the whole attack had stalled within five minutes; but before the advance ground to a halt, some of the Scots had got close enough to the Turkish trenches to start lobbing hand grenades at them. It was almost a waste of time and bravery. Of the 123 grenades thrown, only 43 went off. The problem with the British hand grenades at the time was that they were improvised out of jam tins filled with explosives. The Turks had real, factory-made hand grenades.

The 7th Scottish Rifles were then thrown into the attack and actually managed to gain a small foothold in the Turkish front trench, but fanatical Turkish counter-attacks soon drove the Scots back to their own lines. On the Scottish Rifles' west flank the 7th Royal Scots and 4th Royal Scots managed to capture and hold the Turkish trenches assigned to them. The Royal Scots had more ground cover during their advance and were not exposed to any surprise machine-gun fire from the flank. Further west again, the 29th Division, supported by the artillery and naval gunfire, captured five lines of Turkish trenches and this was enough for Hunter-Weston to declare the battle a British victory. The men of the 29th Division found the Turkish survivors of the British bombardment wandering around their trenches in a daze.

The Turkish High Command, dominated by veteran German officers, blamed the 29th Division's success on the cowardice of the men defending the trenches. An order was issued that any man, officer or not, who left his trench without orders from then on would be executed. General Hamilton blamed the inexperienced Scots for attacking without proper artillery support.

'The attack by the Lowland Division seems to have been mishandled,' he wrote in his diary.

'A brigade made an assault on the east of the Ravine; the men advanced gallantly but there was a lack of effective preparation.

'Two battalions of the Royal Scots carried a couple of the enemy's trenches in fine style and stuck to them, but the rest of the brigade lost a number of good men to no useful purpose in their push against H12.

'One thing is clear. If the bombardment was ineffective, for whatever cause, then the men should not have been allowed to break cover.'

Surely, if he had been doing his job, Hamilton would have known that the Scottish Rifles had no real artillery support and should have prevented their attack going ahead.

The hours after that attack were a nightmare for the men lying badly wounded in No Man's Land and surrounded by thick clouds of buzzing flies. The Turkish machine-guns made rescue impossible. A fire, or possibly several fires, broke out in the parched scrub and grass which covered the battlefield. It slowly crept over swathes of No Man's Land, incinerating the wounded one-by-one.

In most battles the wounded outnumber the dead by three or four-to-one. Roll-call for the 8th Scottish Rifles after the battle showed only one officer out of 26 involved had come through without a scratch; 15 of his colleagues were dead and ten were wounded. The story was the same for the rank and file; they suffered 334 dead and 114 wounded. The 7th Scottish Rifles fared better, reporting 168 dead and 104 wounded. After the battle, the two battalions were amalgamated into one, but there were only enough men left standing to form three rifles companies instead of the standard four companies for a full-strength infantry battalion.

The total casualty figure, dead, wounded and missing, for the British troops involved in the attack at Gully Ravine was in the region of 4,000 men. The Turks lost closer to 12,000 in a seven-day series of futile counter-attacks to recapture the trenches they had lost.

The 52nd Division's commander, Major-General Granville Egerton, was livid at the way his mens' lives had been thrown away. While showing Hamilton and Hunter-Weston around the positions held by the 156 Brigade, he insisted on introducing each of its four battalions as the '... remnants of ...'. On the fourth introduction Hamilton reprimanded Egerton for making remarks within earshot of the soldiers that were detrimental to their morale. By the time of Hamilton's tour, the brigade had lost 1,353 men and it is hard to believe that Egerton's comments hurt morale more than the loss of so many men. Hamilton described the brigade in his diary as 'nice lads' who were feeling 'down on their luck'. And well they might with men like Hamilton and Hunter-Weston in charge. When the division arrived in Gallipoli in mid-June 1915 it had 10,900 men; a month later there were only 6,500 left.

Hunter-Weston was later to remove Egerton from command during a major Turkish attack. If changing horses in midstream is a bad idea, changing generals in mid-battle is usually suicidal. Fortunately for Egerton's successor, the Turkish attack petered out without much more need for his intervention.

Days later the buffoonish Hunter-Weston, who verged on the popular stereotype of a First World War general, collapsed from supposed sunstroke and had himself sent back to Britain. Amazingly, he was then given a senior command on the Western Front. He lost 14,000 men on the first day of the 1916 Somme offensive by the simple expedient of giving the German machine-gunners ten minutes to get out of their shell-proof bunkers and man their weapons after the British artillery stopped firing. The British infantry advancing across No Man's Land were mown down.

When he was told about the slaughter of the 8th Scottish Rifles at Gallipoli, Hunter-Weston demonstrated his trademark nonchalance regarding casualties.

'That will blood the pups,' he declared.

One of those so-called pups was my own great-grandfather. His bones lie in a mass grave somewhere in Gallipoli. I wonder what Private 276 Robert Cowan, or his widow with two young children back in Glasgow, would have made of Hunter-Weston's comment.

COURAGE ALONE IS NOT ENOUGH

ST VALERY 1940

When young Highland lads flocked to join the Territorial Army's 51st Highland Division in the late 1930s, little did they realise many were signing up for five years hard labour in German-occupied Poland as prisoners of war. There was hardly a home in the Highlands and Islands untouched by the Division's surrender at the French seaside town of St Valery-en-Caux in June 1940 after the majority of the British Expeditionary Force had been evacuated from Dunkirk.

The loss of the Division was a source of dismay and bafflement for a British public reared on tales of its fine fighting record during the First World War, when its kilted soldiers had been dubbed by the Germans as 'The Ladies From Hell'.

Hidden behind the bluster and propaganda which marked the outbreak of the Second World War in Britain, however, was the fact that about the only thing the youngsters of the Division had in common with their fathers who fought with it during the First World War was courage.

The British Army was in no state to fight a major war in Europe. By the time the First World War ended in 1918, the 51st Highland Division had become a finely honed fighting machine which used the latest weapons and tactics to smash the Germans. When the Second World War began, the Division was still basically using those same tactics and weapons. The German military machine was planning to fight a far different war.

The British Government had decided to double the size of the part-time Territorial Army as it became increasingly obvious in the late 1930s that a war with Hitler's Germany was almost inevitable. Young men flocked to drill halls across the Highlands and Islands to do their duty for king, country and empire; and for children of the Great Depression of the 1930s, a bit of part-time soldiering offered some welcome extra income. They were proud to wear the uniforms of such famous names from military history as the Seaforth Highlanders, the Gordon Highlanders, the Black Watch and the Argyll and Sutherland Highlanders.

But the Territorial Army was the poor relation of the regular army, and the regular army was the poor relation of the Royal Navy and the Royal Air Force. What money the government was prepared to spend on defence after the First World War, and that wasn't much until the late 1930s, had gone to provide the navy and air force with the most up-to-date equipment available.

The army soldiered on with basically the same rifles and machine-guns that had served it so well during the First World War. Radio communications were poor and British tanks were either fast, but too lightly armoured, or heavy and far too slow. In reality, the German infantry were not much better equipped, but German tactics were far superior. Like most losers in a major conflict, the Germans had sat down after the First World War and taken a hard look at what had gone wrong. They learned lessons which the British and French ignored after the war and came up with an approach which integrated their tanks with airpower, particularly their dreaded Stuka dive-bombers, and highly mobile artillery. This combination allowed them to drive fast and deep through enemy lines – Blitzkrieg.

Meanwhile, much of the British Army was still living in the 19th century. The generals still believed the best officers were drawn from the 'better class of person'. It was out of the question for a duke, say the Duke of Argyll, to serve as a private; he had to be an

officer. The same was true for nearly all the battalions in the 51st
Highland Division, where officer status was almost automatically
given to local members of the minor gentry and other 'community
leaders'. It was not an atmosphere that encouraged innovative
thought or even a high level of professionalism when it came to
soldiering.

When the fighting began in France, very basic practices, such
as scouting out the location of the enemy positions before a battle,
were seldom carried out. The ordinary soldiers tended to confuse
sensible tactics with cowardice, and would charge straight for
German machine-guns when they should have employed more
devious approaches to dealing with them – approaches that British
troops in the latter stages of the war used almost without thinking.
The Highland Division in 1940 was to pay very heavily for its lack
of practical training. That lack of training before the war was partly
due to the scattered nature of the division's troops across the
Highlands and Islands which made it harder to bring the men
together than in the more densely populated areas where the other
Territorial battalions operated.

After the Second World War began, concerns about the
suitability of the part-time soldiers for battle led to a decision to
swap three of its nine battalions for regular soldiers from the
Seaforths, Gordons and Black Watch. However, the regular British
Army was not in a much better state than the Territorial Army. Years
of government underspending had reduced the army to little more
than a force fit only to keep order in the British Empire. In the years
leading up to the Second World War there was no major exercise
held which would have prepared troops to fight in a modern large-
scale European war. In 1938 the regulars of the 1st Black Watch went
on exercise with only 300 men, no mortars and no anti-tank guns.

The British Army was marginally smaller than the Dutch and
less than half the strength of the Belgian Army. It was only after the
war began that the British gave much thought to considering
natural leadership ability, rather than a family's wealth and social
status, as the main qualification for becoming an officer. The rank

and file were mainly drawn from deprived urban areas and many entered the army physically under-developed and with appallingly poor educations. It has been said that throughout the war German troops showed far more personal initiative during the fighting than their British counter-parts.

Few European nations took the British Army seriously. Britain could only send 150,000 men to fight alongside 2.7 million Frenchmen against the Germans. Sending British troops into continental Europe was more of a political gesture than a genuine military contribution to the war. That meant that being seen to support the French took priority over purely military considerations.

One of the ways of demonstrating solidarity with the French was to put British troops under French command and the 51st Highland Division was chosen for this dubious honour. Even if the Division's commander, Major-General Victor Fortune, had not been ordered by London to stick with the French through thick and thin for political reasons, he probably would have anyway; Fortune was a very loyal man.

The Division's first assignment under French command was to help garrison the legendary Maginot Line of massive concrete forts along the French-German border. The French had pinned a lot of faith in the Maginot Line and its network of interlocking artillery and machine-gun posts. Sadly, the line did not extend along the French-Belgian border and the German invasion on 10 May 1940, came through Belgium. The Germans had opened the First World War by attacking France via Belgium, so the move was not unexpected. But, the French High Command positioned their troops to repel a German attack across the plains of Flanders while the Panzer divisions were actually coming through the Ardennes, a wooded mountainous region the French believed was impassable for tanks.

The emergence of the German tanks from the Ardennes reduced the defence plans of the French to chaos. French troops were outflanked and outmanoeuvred by the fast-moving German tank columns while Gort and the main British army headed for the Channel coast as quickly as possible; genuine co-operation between the French and British was almost non-existent. The British accused the French of collapsing like a wet paper bag in the face of the Germans, while the French said that the British could not get away from the Germans quickly enough.

Gort attempted only one major counter-attack against the Germans. His action near Arras with 74 of his best tanks took the Germans by surprise, but it was broken off after 46 of the tanks were destroyed. Gort was soon heading for the coast again and the new British Prime Minister, Winston Churchill, was dealing with an outraged French Government.

Churchill was determined, in view of Gort's continued retreat, that the Highland Division would be seen to stand by the French. It had been helping deal with a diversionary attack by the Germans on the Maginot Line, but on 20 May was pulled back to help defend Paris. It continued to retreat in lock step with the French to a defence line being improvised along the River Somme. It was here that the Division suffered almost 600 casualties on 4 June, when it was thrown into a battle near Abbeville aimed at pushing the Germans out of a bridgehead they had formed on the west bank of the Somme. Poor co-operation between the French tanks and the Highland infantry was blamed for the failed counter-attack.

The Division had its own tanks, from the Lothian and Borders Horse, but their armour was too light for them to be much use in a full battle. It was also supported by artillery batteries and two English machine-gun battalions, from the Royal Northumberland Fusiliers and the Princess Louise's Kensington Regiment. When medics, transport corps drivers, engineers and other support troops are factored in, it becomes clear that St Valery was very far from a purely Scottish tragedy. Scots provided the bulk of the Division's infantry, but infantry only made up around 2,500 of the 8,000 troops captured at St Valery.

The infantry had suffered heavily during the retreat to the seaside town. They were seldom out of range of the German artillery and mortars. German aircraft frequently swept down out of the skies to machine-gun and bomb the long columns of retreating soldiers and civilians which were choking the narrow roads of northern France at the time. Many survivors of the retreat who served with the Division spoke later of the piles of dead women and children they saw along the sides of roads.

For the Highland soldiers, the week-long retreat was a constant round of marching, digging protective trenches and then more marching. At rest stops many of the infantrymen fell asleep where they had slumped to the ground and had to be punched and kicked awake again when the time came to resume marching.

The Division headed for Dieppe where it was expected the Royal Navy would evacuate them back to Britain. But before the Highlanders could reach the town, it was decided to block the harbour mouth with sunken ships to prevent it being used by the Germans. Fortune was then told to take his men to Le Havre for evacuation, but only two badly-mauled battalions of Argylls and a battalion of Black Watch soldiers reached the port before the German tank columns cut off their escape route.

The Royal Navy got the men who reached Le Havre away safely and it was then suggested that the rest of the Division make for St Valery, 20 miles west of Dieppe, for evacuation. St Valery was far from a perfect spot for an evacuation, but it was now the Division's only hope. The harbour there was difficult for ships to get in and out of and the approaches to it could easily be dominated by artillery guns placed on the hills and coastal cliffs around it.

The bulk of the Division reached St Valery on 11 June; they were a day too late. The Royal Navy had nosed its ships into the harbour the night before but had to leave before dawn to avoid becoming sitting ducks for German bombers. Thick fog prevented them from returning to the harbour after dark on June 11 and the Highland infantry defending the hills around the town were told they would have to hold for one more day for the planned evacuation.

The German commander, Major-General Erwin Rommel, had

no intention of giving the British another day. He pushed his commanders to drive the Highlanders off the high ground that dominated the town as quickly as possible. The Scots had little more than courage to hold back the German tanks. The anti-tank rifles they had been issued were inadequate and their positions were plastered by mortar fire. Much-needed ammunition supplies had been destroyed in anticipation of the naval evacuation to prevent them falling into German hands. Now the Navy was not coming for them after all and the defenders needed the ammunition.

Despite all the handicaps, the infantry doggedly held onto the hills. It took the personal intervention of Rommel at the head of the 25th Panzer Regiment to drive the Highlanders from the high ground north-west of the town. Then, once the German artillery was set up, it was impossible for the Royal Navy to enter the harbour and the bulk of the Highland Division was trapped. Around 1,350 British and 930 French were evacuated by the navy from nearby beaches, some of them only accessible by climbing down 300-ft cliffs using ropes improvised by joining rifle slings together.

Back in the town, nearly every house was burning as the Germans lobbed in an estimated 2,500 high-explosive shells from their new positions on the high ground. French troops began surrendering in droves, but Fortune ignored an order from the local French commander to surrender. On the morning of 12 June he bowed to the inevitable to avoid any further loss of his soldiers' lives and surrendered. It took a couple of hours to persuade the Highlanders dug in east of town for a last stand that the surrender order was genuine. Many of Fortune's men in the town tried to go into hiding but French civilians led the Germans straight to them.*

After the Division surrendered, Fortune was very sick and the Germans offered to return him to Britain as part of a prisoner exchange. But Fortune refused to leave behind the men he had led

* A plan in the 1980s to twin the Highland capital of Inverness with St Valery had little support from the veterans who had fought there, but local politicians went ahead with the arrangement anyway.

into captivity and he remained a prisoner for the entire war. Fortune extended the same brand of loyalty to the French. When the bulk of the British Army under General Lord Gort pretty much abandoned the French to the advancing Germans, Fortune could easily have done the same. The Division had enough trucks to carry its men rapidly to the Channel coast but that would have meant deserting the far less mobile French 31st Division and leaving it to be torn apart by the German Panzer divisions. That was something Fortune would just not do.

The surrender was a bitter pill to swallow for young men who were intent on upholding the reputation their fathers had earned for the Division during the First World War; many refused to accept captivity. Out of 290 British soldiers who escaped from the Germans while being held as prisoners of war up until June 1941, 134 were from the 51st Highland Division.

The pill became even more bitter when letters from baffled relatives in Britain arrived at the prisoner of war camps in German-occupied Poland via the Red Cross accusing the young soldiers of cowardice. The real story of surrender, which involved the complete inadequacy of the British army in the opening phases of the war, could not be told without damaging morale back home.

But the British Government decided that the 51st Highland Division was too good a brand name to lose. A new 51st Highland Division was created from two of the three battalions which had been evacuated from Le Havre and by breaking up another Territorial Division, the 9th Scottish Division, to provide replacement battalions. The disbandment of the 9th Scottish Division must have hurt its veterans from the First World War because it probably had an even better war record than the more glamorous all-kilted 51st Highland Division.

However, the new combination upheld the traditions of both its First World War predecessors. The resurrected Highland Division was the only major British unit to fight under the command of Field Marshal Bernard Montgomery all the way from his victory in the Western Desert over their nemesis at St Valery,

Rommel, to the final battles in Germany which ended in the war in Europe in May 1945. Apart from a brief period after the D-Day landings in 1944 when it appeared to have lost its edge, the Highland Division was always trusted at the fore of the fighting.

Montgomery made sure it was the Highland Division that had the honour of liberating St Valery from the Germans in 1944, but how much comfort that was to the men who still faced several months of slave bondage on Polish farms and down that country's coal mines before the war finally ended is debatable.

A long number of years were to pass before many of the original heroes of St Valery could bring themselves to talk about the horror and humiliation of those dark days during the summer of 1940.

THE FIGHTING FRENCH

LEBANON 1941

Britain's war against France during the Second World War does not get a big billing in most histories of the conflict. Maybe that is why so few have heard about the disaster which befell No 11 (Scottish) Commando in what is now Lebanon during the summer of 1941. After France surrendered to the Germans and Italians in 1940, the French were allowed to continue governing their colonies in Africa, the Middle East, and Indo-China from the unoccupied city of Vichy in the south of the country. But Britain and its Commonwealth allies had major concerns about how far the government in Vichy would go to appease the Germans.

One of the most important French colonies in the world from a British point of view was Syria. It bordered oil-rich Iraq and offered an excellent base for a German invasion of that country. Syria also offered a backdoor route for a German invasion of Egypt and the Suez Canal. The Germans under Lieutenant-General Erwin Rommel were already pushing across the desert towards the canal from the west.

By early 1941 the British were very concerned about German activity in both Syria and Iraq. A pro-Nazi coup in Iraq led to the British-held airfield at Habbaniya being besieged by Iraqi troops. Not only that, but German planes bearing Iraqi insignia had been using bases in Syria to bomb the British airfield.

The Vichy French Governor of Syria, General Henri Dentz,

found himself in a very delicate position as his political masters became increasingly keen to please the Germans. Some of his troops had already deserted to join the pro-Allied Free French under the command of General Charles De Gaulle. Once the British had defeated the pro-Nazi regime in Iraq and installed a more friendly government, they turned their attention to Syria.

The fight in the Western Desert against Rommel's Afrika Korps was using up most of the British troops in the Middle East, but it was decided that a division of Australian troops could be spared for the invasion of Syria. The successful seizure of the road bridge over the Litani River, now in present-day Lebanon, seemed crucial to the invasion and No. 11 (Scottish) Commando was given the job.

It was one of two commando units recruited from volunteers serving in the Scottish Command area in July 1940 and had yet to see action as a unit. Its men had trained in Scotland for several months and wore Scottish Tam o'Shanters with black hackles to distinguish themselves from other commando units. Although proud of its Scottish links, the Commando was by no means exclusively made up of Scots soldiers. Amongst its officers was Ulsterman Lieutenant Paddy Mayne, who would go on to become a key figure in the founding of the Special Air Service.

The Seaforths, Gordons, Black Watch and Camerons were all well represented in the new unit and there were also a number of soldiers from the Nottinghamshire-based 9th Battalion of the Sherwood Foresters and the Royal Artillery. The Commando was under the command of Lieutenant-Colonel Dick Pedder of the Highland Light Infantry; he was strict disciplinarian who was feared and detested by many of his men. However, he instilled a high level of military professionalism and physical fitness during the unit's training in Galashiels and Arran.

Pedder insisted on his men marching the 100 miles from Galashiels to Ayr before the move to Arran for further training. One of the men who failed to complete the march was Captain Geoffrey Keyes of the Royal Scots Greys. This should have meant that Keyes was kicked out of the Commando, but he was special. His father, Admiral Sir John Keyes, was Director of Combined Operations, the effective boss of all British commando forces. One of the admiral's first moves was to have his son posted to No 11 Commando. Geoffrey Keyes was no-one's idea of a commando. He had curvature of the spine, poor hearing and eyesight and was regarded as unpredictable and inconsistent. However, there was no way Pedder could afford to alienate his boss and Keyes was sent ahead on a baggage truck to Ayr after struggling badly on the first day of the march from Galashiels.

After completing their training on Arran, the Scottish Commando was sent to the Mediterranean along with No 7 and No 8 Commandos. For security reasons each of the Commandos was given a letter of the alphabet and No 11 became known as C Battalion of a mysterious outfit christened Layforce. The Scots commandos were sent to garrison Cyprus, while A Battalion and B Battalion went to Crete where they were badly mauled in the successful German invasion of the island.

The plan for the seizure of the Litani Bridge involved a commando attack to coincide with the Australian 7th Division crossing the border from British-held Palestine into what was then still part of Syria. The commando landing was scheduled for 7 June, but due to heavy surf on the beach and obvious heavy French patrol activity in the area, the Royal Navy called it off. The cancellation gave the French time to blow the bridge before the advancing Australians could reach it. It was soon obvious that the French intended to fight the invaders.

Following the destruction of the bridge, a new plan was developed. It called for the commandos to land on the north side of the river mouth and drive the French defenders, men of the Algerian 22nd Tirailleurs, away, while the Australians built a pontoon bridge across it.

The main attack on the French positions north of the river was entrusted to Keyes, now a major, with 140 commandos. He had brought a number of volunteers to the Commando from his old unit, the Royal Scots Greys, and liked to refer to them as his 'Cavaliers'. For the attack at Litani his force was dubbed 'X Party'.

Pedder was to land with 150 men on the coast a few miles north of Keyes's group and capture the main French barracks in the area; his group was christened 'Y Party'. Finally, a third group of just over 100 men under Captain George More, known as 'Z Party' was to be put ashore four miles north of the river mouth; their mission was to capture the Kafr Badda Bridge over a stream north of the main fighting and prevent French reinforcements from reaching the Algerian troops.

The landings began around 3am on 9 June and by 4.20am Pedder and More's men were ashore. Captain More lost his radios when the landing craft carrying them was holed by an offshore rock and took on water. However, the real disaster happened further south. Keyes and his men were landed on the south side of the river by mistake. One of the commandos realised that the Navy had got it wrong, but his protests were ignored and they were put ashore. The confusion was caused by a sandbank which hid the mouth of the river and the fact that there were two almost identical farmhouses on either bank.

The commandos moved inland to find the Australians were ahead of them and preparing an attack across the river. Now, instead of attacking the French machine-gun and artillery positions guarding the river crossing from behind and in the dark, Keyes decided to launch a frontal attack across the river in broad daylight.

The French were soon plastering the British and Australian troops south of the river with their machine-guns, 75mm artillery and 81mm heavy mortars. Keyes borrowed some boats from the Australians and tried to get his men across the river, but they were met by a hail of French machine-gun fire. By 10am only six of the commandos were on the north bank.

In the meantime, about 40 of Keyes's men had become separated and decided to put themselves under Australian command. Gradually, the commandos managed to slip across the river despite the French fire and by 12.30pm they had about 14 men on the north bank. They managed to capture a small 25mm anti-tank gun which they used to knock-out one of the French 75mm artillery guns.

The main French machine-gun position covering the site of the now demolished bridge had come under heavy artillery fire from the Australians and ran up a white flag around lunchtime. By 9pm the Australians had managed to get a large number of their men across to the north bank and they linked up with Keyes's men. However, the Australian crossing came too late for many of Pedder and More's men who already had been killed or captured.

Both groups had started out well, but, without the support they expected from Keyes and his men, they were eventually surrounded and overwhelmed by determined French counter-attacks. More's men quickly overran the French positions near the coast and pushed inland to capture an artillery position and some transport trucks. By 6am they were in possession of the Kafr Badda Bridge. The French troops assigned to defend the bridge had retreated to a stronger position 300 yards further north.

Mid-morning saw the arrival of eight French armoured cars which started pounding the commandos with their two-pounder cannon and machine-guns. The Scots managed to hold them off until 4pm when six more armoured cars showed up and it was obvious they were about to be overwhelmed. More tried to lead about two dozen of his men back to the beach, but they found their way blocked by barbed wire. The French caught up with the fugitives and opened fire with machine-guns. To make matters worse, the Australians on the south bank mistook the commandos for French troops and also started firing their machine-guns at them.

After suffering five dead and three wounded, Captain More decided to surrender. His party was taken to a farm called Aiteniye where they spent the night as prisoners of the French. In the morning the French realised that they were about to be overrun by the Australians, who were now across the Litani in strength, and decided to surrender to More. The captives had become captors.

The men from More's group who decided not to follow him in

his bid to reach the beach again managed to head inland and evade capture until the Australians arrived.

Pedder and his men were landed in waist-deep water and waded ashore in the face of heavy machine-gun fire from the French manning the beach defences; surprisingly, they suffered only one casualty. Once on land, they followed a dried-up stream bed towards the French barracks they had been assigned to capture. They seized a French ammunition dump on the way, but then became pinned down by machine-gun and sniper fire. Pedder, a tough taskmaster who refused to suffer fools gladly, was killed by a bullet in the back and all the other officers in the group were wounded. The Regimental Sergeant Major, Lewis Tevendale, took command and tried to organise a retreat but the French had them too well pinned down. At around 5pm the commandos surrendered.

During the early stages of the fighting, some of Pedder's troops, mainly men who had joined the Commando from the Royal Artillery, managed to capture a French 75mm gun manned by Senegalese troops from Africa and use it to destroy three more French artillery pieces nearby. The British gunners then made their way back to Pedder's position. Lieutenant Paddy Mayne and his troop of 30 commandos had been following Pedder's group towards the barracks but got cut off. They managed to capture just under 100 French soldiers before coming under fire from both the Algerians and the Australians. Mayne and his men made their way back to the Litani River where they hid until next morning. Then they crossed to the south bank over the new Australian pontoon bridge to rejoin the main Commonwealth contingent. The whole operation had cost No 11 Commando 40 dead and 80 wounded out of an original force of just under 400 men.

Following Pedder's death, Keyes was made commanding officer of the Commando. But it was not a happy unit. Mayne and a fellow former officer from the Royal Ulster Rifles left to become among the first members of a new outfit recruiting in the Middle East, the Special Air Service. Legend has it that Mayne was forced to leave No 11 Commando after punching Keyes, but that is probably all part of the myth-making process which surrounded the early days of the SAS. It is more likely that Mayne was persuaded to move on after the Commando's Major Charles Napier reported being viciously attacked in the dark by a mystery assailant; shortly before the assault, Napier had reprimanded Mayne for his drunken behaviour at a function. Mayne would go on to command an SAS battalion in northern Europe in the latter stages of the war.

No replacements were sent out from Britain to make up for the men lost at Litani or for the other two Commando units to replace the men killed and captured in Crete; it was decided to merge all three Commandos into one unit. However, when Keyes asked for volunteers from No 11 Commando to join the new composite Commando, only five officers and 110 men stepped forward out of the possible nine officers and 250 men available.

Keyes was killed in November 1941 during an attempt to kill Rommel at his headquarters in Libya. Accounts of the raid are contradictory and confused, but it now seems likely that Keyes was accidentally shot by a fellow officer inside the building which had been wrongly identified as Rommel's headquarters. The officer was himself shot in the leg minutes later by another of the raiders. The raid was a waste of time not only because the building was no longer used by Rommel, but also because the German general was in Italy at the time. Despite the raid's failure and serious question marks over the way it was conducted, Keyes was awarded a posthumous Victoria Cross.

The Allied force attacking Syria was reinforced after the fighting on the Litani and General Dentz finally surrendered on 14 July. His army of 38,000 troops was given the choice of being sent to another piece of Vichy-controlled territory or joining the Free French forces fighting alongside the Allies. Less than 6,000 opted to fight for General De Gaulle's Free French.

France went on to be honoured for its war effort and was even given an occupation zone in Germany when the fighting was over. People did not talk much about the Scottish soldiers killed by the French.

THE FLEET OF FOOT

HONG KONG 1941

There is an old saying about there being no bad dogs – just bad owners. The army has a similar saying relating to soldiers and officers and in the Hong Kong of 1941 that piece of folk wisdom had particular relevance for the 2nd Battalion of the Royal Scots. The battalion had two problems. The first was that many of its officers were not at the top of their game. The second was that they had been given an impossible job. Hong Kong could not be held for long in the face of its expected invasion by Japanese troops.

British wartime Prime Minister Winston Churchill himself had declared that there was 'not the slightest chance' of holding Hong Kong if the Japanese chose to invade. In the closing months of 1941 that invasion was looking more and more likely. The Japanese had been fighting in China since 1931 and, in an attempt to curb Japan's expansionist policies, the United States had imposed an oil embargo on the island nation. Japan's leadership decided to attack the USA while they still had some oil reserves left.

Short of direct military intervention the United States had been very supportive of the British in their war against Hitler's Germany and the Japanese realised that Britain would ally itself with the Americans against Japan. That meant the Japanese would have to capture the strategically important British naval base at Hong Kong. The war in Europe had stretched British military resources almost to breaking point and few troops could be spared to fight the Japanese in the Far East. It was decided to concentrate the troops at the supposedly impregnable island fortress of Singapore at the tip of the Malaya peninsula and leave only a token garrison at Hong Kong.

The Royal Scots were part of that token garrison. They had been stationed in the Crown Colony since 1938 and life was good there for soldiers brought up in the slums of Edinburgh and the grim mining towns of West Lothian. Beer and entertainment were cheap.

The Japanese had been drawing up plans to invade Hong Kong for years and the colony was swarming with their spies. Japanese barbers, actually intelligence officers, worked in all the best hotels offering fantastically cheap haircuts. Japanese prostitutes made British servicemen particularly welcome. When the Japanese attack came in December 1941 they had plans for almost all the British defensive positions in their path and had even been conducting training with mock-ups of some of the key ones.

While the Japanese were preparing for war, the officers of the Royal Scots were busy having a good time. Training was looked on as an unwelcome intrusion into the constant round of parties hosted by the British business community. Senior British officers had major concerns about the battalion's readiness for war. High levels of sexually transmitted diseases and malaria among the Scots soldiers were taken to indicate a lack of competence among the battalion's officers. The rate at which officers and men from the Royal Scots were being court-martialled also raised warning flags at the Hong Kong garrison's headquarters. Confidential reports dismissed the senior officers in the Royal Scots as useless and traced the start of the rot in fighting efficiency to a previous commanding officer who was regarded as a gin-sodden wreck.

On the eve of the Japanese invasion, 7 December, the battalion was commanded by Lieutenant-Colonel Simon White. He was thought of as a pleasant man, but not up to restoring the battalion's reputation. A move to replace him came to nothing because no other officer in the battalion could be found who was thought capable of doing a better job. White had an added headache to deal with. The rapid expansion of the British army in the last few years leading up to the Second World War had seen the battalion robbed of many of its best and most experienced soldiers to train new recruits back in the United Kingdom.

Considering the low regard the battalion was held in, it may be a surprise to learn that the Royal Scots were given a key position to hold in the defensive line. The plans for the defence of Hong Kong changed on an almost annual basis; one year, the defence plan was based on a defence of the colony's mainland territories, and the next year only Hong Kong Island itself was to be defended. The defence plan was usually linked to how many soldiers were available.

In late 1941 the garrison commander, Major-General Christopher Maltby, decided he had only enough men to defend the island. However, the British Imperial Defence Staff then decided two battalions of raw and barely trained Canadian troops could be spared to reinforce the garrison at Hong Kong. This raised the number of battalions available to Maltby from four to six and he decided to hold an 11-mile-long defensive position on the mainland known as the Gin Drinkers' Line.

But the troops would be so thinly spread that Maltby did not expect that they would be able to do more than delay the Japanese advance for more than a week or so. As things turned out, even that proved optimistic. The line ran along a series of hills and in previous years, as part of past defence plans, some concrete bunkers had been constructed on them.

Unfortunately, Maltby was underestimating the strength of the Japanese force preparing to invade Hong Kong. Maltby had 14,000 men to do a job which military analysts calculated needed three times that number. The Japanese had 60,000 men earmarked for the invasion. The British had 2,000 men on the Gin Drinkers' Line; the Japanese assigned 10,000 for its capture. Standard military wisdom suggested an attacking force should outnumber the defenders by three-to-one. The Japanese had a five-to-one superiority.

The Royal Scots were ordered to hold the key Shing Mun Redoubt on the Gin Drinkers' Line. The use of the word 'redoubt' gives an impression of defensive strength which is not justified. The position consisted of five bunkers spread positioned across 12 acres of bare hillside and linked by trenches and concrete tunnels. The bunkers were badly sited and could not provide mutual covering fire. There were also some blind spots in their fields of view which Japanese troops could use to creep into the heart of the bunker complex undetected. Worst of all, there were not enough troops manning the bunkers. The Japanese believed the British would have at least 100 men manning the Shing Mun position, but the Royal Scots had only 40.

The Scots were commanded by Captain 'Potato' Jones, a legendary party animal in pre-war Hong Kong. He was later to be strongly criticised for failing to send out adequate patrols, which senior British officers believed would have spotted the advancing Japanese sooner.

The Japanese offensive to capture Hong Kong was timed to coincide with the surprise attack on the US Pacific Fleet at its anchorage at Pearl Harbour in Hawaii. The date in Hong Kong was 8 December; the Japanese opened their attack on Hong Kong by bombing the airfield which was home to the colony's air defences. Two of the three obsolete Vilderbeeste torpedo biplanes which comprised the air defence were put out of action and the colony's only two seaplanes were sunk at their harbour moorings in the same raid.

By nightfall the following day the Japanese were ready to attack the Shing Mun Redoubt. A force of 150 men wearing rubber-soled boots began creeping silently up the hill, but they were spotted around 11pm by a corporal who opened fire with his Thompson submachine-gun. A heavier Vickers medium machine-gun joined in and briefly checked the Japanese advance.

The Japanese, many of them veterans of several years of fighting in China, were soon swarming over the bunkers. The majority of the Scots found themselves trapped underground, although one group of them did stage a counter-attack which was thrown back by the Japanese. British artillery guns then opened fire in a bid to drive the Japanese off the hill, but they only succeeded in hitting one of the

British bunkers and burying its occupants alive. The Japanese dug the Scottish soldiers out next morning.

In the confusion 13 of the defenders managed to reach temporary safety in nearby British positions. The Japanese captured 28 British soldiers at Shing Mun. The total of three defenders killed does not suggest many gallant last stands or a particularly vigorous effort. Elsewhere in the sector held by the Royal Scots, news of the loss of Shing Mun sent the men heading for the rear. Lieutenant-Colonel White was ordered by headquarters to organise a counter-attack, but all he did was offer excuses before pulling the battalion back two miles to a position on Golden Hill.

Golden Hill was not an easy position to hold; some trenches had been dug there years before, but successive monsoon rains had collapsed them. The Royal Scots on the hill had little protection from the hail of mortar shells the Japanese began plastering their positions with on 10 December. The ground was concrete-hard because of the midwinter freeze and the solid lumps of earth thrown up by the mortar-bomb explosions were as dangerous as any shrapnel. The British had little mortar ammunition to fire back in reply to the Japanese bombardment.

The Japanese sent their infantry, masters of camouflage, sneaking forward under cover of the mortar fire until they were about 100 feet from the Royal Scots' positions. Then they rose, apparently out of the soil, for a bayonet charge. The Scots fled. White was unable to explain to garrison headquarters why two companies of his men were retreating.

A third company, under Captain David Pinkerton, launched a successful counter-attack and drove the Japanese back off Golden Hill. But without reinforcements, he was forced to withdraw when the Japanese attacked again. Pinkerton survived the war, only to die from a stray bullet during the British invasion of the Suez Canal region of Egypt in 1956.

The Royal Scots lost 29 men at Golden Hill. But they also lost something more. The Royal Scots were proud of their position as the premier infantry regiment in the British army. Only the Brigade of

Guards had precedence over them, and they rejoiced in being known as 'The First of Foot'. Following their poor performance on the Gin Drinkers' Line, the cheery cockneys of the Hong Kong Garrison's 1st Middlesex Regiment now dubbed the Scots as 'The Fleet of Foot'.

The capture of Shing Mún meant that the Gin Drinkers' Line could not be held and the mainland New Territories were lost. The Royal Scots were loaded onto buses after their retreat from Golden Hill and taken down to the docks where they were put onto the ferries which carried them across to Hong Kong Island.

The defence of the island lasted until Christmas Day 1941 when the British finally surrendered in the face of overwhelming odds. The Royal Scots did much to redeem their reputation during the fighting on the island and by the time of the surrender only four officers and 85 men from the battalion's original strength of 700 were still standing.

Japanese troops had been engaging in an orgy of slaughter, pillage and rape even before the final British surrender. The Japanese 228th Regiment, which had captured Shing Mun, was particularly guilty of murdering prisoners in cold blood and no-one will ever know how many Hong Kong Chinese civilians died at the hands of their new masters. Nurses were singled out for rape and later murdered. The soldiers, white civilians and nurses who survived spent three-and-a-half years in Japanese prisoner camps, where many more were worked to death, starved or executed. Thousands of those who survived to be released from the Japanese camps at the end of the war never fully recovered from the bestial treatment inflicted on them.

Fate had one last trick to play on the Royal Scots after the Christmas Day surrender. A ship, the *Lisbon Maru*, carrying 1,800 British prisoners, many of them Scots, from Hong Kong was torpedoed by a US submarine in October 1942. The Japanese abandoned the ship, but not before locking the prisoners below decks; only half the prisoners managed to escape from the sinking ship. They were picked up out of the water by the Japanese and continued their journey towards the hell of Japanese captivity.

THE COSSACKS

AUSTRIA 1945

The men of the 8th Argyll and Sutherland Highlanders had had a rough ride during the Second World War – and after Germany's surrender in 1945 they were caught up in one last terrible tragedy. The Scottish soldiers were used to force thousands of Russian Cossacks who had fought in the German army, along with their families, back to the Soviet Union. There the Cossacks faced instant execution or a lingering death in slave camps. Hundreds would die during the repatriation. The process of sending the Cossacks to the Soviet Occupation Zone was both violent and heartbreaking as the Scots, wielding pickaxe handles and rifle butts, waded into a crowd of hysterical men, women and children desperate to avoid the move.

The Cossacks had come to regard the Scots who guarded them that long, hot, early summer in 1945 as their friends, but after their forced return to the Soviet Union the Argylls' name became poison on their lips. The bulk Cossacks in the Ukraine had been bitter enemies of the Soviet Red Army since the Russian Revolution in 1917. After the Bolsheviks won the civil war which followed, many of the Cossack leaders fled to Western Europe as refugees.

Hitler's 1941 invasion of the Soviet Union, 20 years after the civil war ended, appeared to offer fresh hope of ridding the Ukraine of its Communist overlords. The exiled Cossacks proved enthusiastic recruiters for a Russian force being raised to fight alongside the

Germans against the Red Army. Cossacks were recruited from prisoner of war camps and the Ukraine, which was occupied by the Germans for a time.

Soviet leader Joseph Stalin was hated in the Ukraine, where his forced collectivisation of farming had caused a famine which had claimed the lives of hundreds of thousands of men, women and children. Before the Russian Revolution, the Cossacks had enjoyed a special status in Russian society. They provided the Czar with ferocious mounted troops who had few qualms about riding down their master's supposed enemies – be they revolutionary crowds in St Petersburg or Jews in Poland; but all that ended with the Russian Revolution.

During the Second World War the Germans found the same use for the Cossacks as the old Czarist regime had. They were sent to various parts of German-occupied Europe to track down and destroy resistance groups. When the Red Army pushed the Germans out of the Ukraine, Hitler promised the Cossacks a new homeland in northern Italy if they would continue to fight for him. As the Second World War drew to a close, the Cossacks retreated into Austria to escape the clutches of vengeful Italian resistance fighters. In Austria, they surrendered to the British Eighth Army on 8 May.

The Cossacks seemed confident that they would be treated as ordinary prisoners of war until what they regarded as the inevitable war between the Western Allies and the Soviet Union broke out. Then they would fight alongside the British and Americans against the Red Army.

What the Cossacks did not know was that Stalin had reached an agreement with British Prime Minister Winston Churchill and US President Franklin Roosevelt in February 1945 that they would be sent back to the Soviet Union. The actual agreement only covered Soviet citizens and not the 500 senior Cossack officers who fled the Ukraine towards the end of the Civil War; but that, as it turned out, did not matter to the British.

The soldiers were under orders from their political masters, anxious not to offend the Soviets, to send everyone back, by hook or by crook. Soviet secret police records claim some very senior Cossack generals were handed over by a British lieutenant-colonel who was told he could keep their stash of 30 pounds of gold bullion in return for his assistance.

At the time it looked to the British that they had several good reasons to appease Stalin. The Red Army had overrun several large prisoner of war camps in Poland which contained British troops and there were fears they would be held hostage until the Cossacks were sent to the Soviet Union. Also, the Western Allies were still fighting the Japanese in the Far East and were anxious for the Soviets to join the fighting on their side. And after all, the Cossacks had collaborated with the Nazis.

The way the British treated the Cossacks contrasts with how Indian troops who fought for the Japanese were handled. The former members of the pro-Japanese Indian National army were dealt with leniently for fear of alienating Indian public opinion in the run up to their independence from Britain in August 1947.

When the British first learned that approximately 30,000 Cossacks had crossed into Austria carrying everything they owned, heavy fighting was anticipated. But instead, the Cossacks meekly surrendered and declared they had no argument with the British and Americans. The bulk of the Cossacks and their families were moved to a meadow near the Austrian city of Lienz, where an old army base formed the nucleus of their encampment. They were joined by other refugees of Russian origin who had taken no part in the war. The Cossack officers were allowed to keep their pistols and were made responsible for the discipline and day-to-day running of the camp. The encampment at Lienz was in the war-weary 8th Argyll and Sutherland Highlanders' area of responsibility.

The battalion was a pre-war Territorial Army part-time unit which drew its recruits from Argyllshire and first saw action in France in 1940 as part of the famed 51st Highland Division. It had taken a hammering when the Germans swept through France and it missed out on the legendary evacuation at Dunkirk. Instead, the survivors of the battalion had escaped back to Britain from Le Havre.

After being brought back up to strength, the battalion had been sent to North Africa as part of the 78th Division. It suffered heavy casualties when it successfully stormed the almost impregnable German positions on Longstop Hill, which had been holding up the Allied advance in Tunisia. The battalion was rebuilt again and sent to Italy where it was part of the Eighth Army's long brutal slog north against successive lines of German strong points all the way to the Austrian border.

After all that, Lienz was idyllic. The Cossacks showed off their horsemanship and dancing skills to the Scots, who were looked on as natural allies; camels kept by the Cossacks added to the carnival atmosphere of the encampment. The Scottish troops shared their chocolate rations with the hordes of children who swarmed around the Cossack camp.

Neither the Scots nor the Cossacks knew of the great betrayal which had been agreed by the politicians. The British generals had decided to keep their troops in the dark about the repatriation plan until the last moment. It was only on 26 May that the first inkling came that something was wrong when the Argylls' officers were ordered to remind their men that the Cossacks were former enemy combatants and not friends.

All of the Cossacks' weapons were confiscated on the pretext that British ones were being issued to them and their 1,500 officers were invited to a mass conference to discuss their future, but there was no conference. The British only wanted to split the officers from their men.

Some Cossack officers smelled a rat immediately and slipped out of the encampment when they heard of the conference. They quickly merged into the masses of refugees roaming Europe at the time. Sympathetic British officers dropped hints that the conference was bogus and may even have helped some of the Cossacks escape. Any doubts about what was really going on evaporated on the day of the supposed conference on 28 May when the transport provided was accompanied by a very heavily armed escort. Instead of any conference, the officers were taken to a prison camp where they were informed that they would be handed over to the Red Army the next day.

Protests from the 500 officers who had never been Soviet citizens were brushed aside. Stalin and his henchmen had made it clear that these were the men in British custody that they were keenest to get their hands on. The Soviets had scores to settle that dated back more than two decades. Several of the Cossack officers committed suicide at the prison camp before they could be handed over. Others worked on futile petitions to Winston Churchill, King George VI, the Red Cross and the United Nations. They asked for a fair trial and claimed, correctly, that they faced mass execution after they were handed over to the Red Army.

On the morning of the handover, the Cossacks refused to board the trucks provided. A platoon from an English regiment was sent to force some of the most senior officers onto the trucks. It turned into a bloody struggle with many of the Cossacks, some well over 60 years old, being beaten senseless with rifle butts and pickaxe handles.

The display of ruthlessness and determination from the British had its desired effect and the rest of the Cossack officers boarded the trucks quietly. However, at the bridge where the handover was taking place there was more bloodshed. One Cossack officer threw himself off the bridge onto the rocks 100 feet below. He was retrieved and handed over to the Soviets. Another officer slit his own throat and fell dying at the feet of a British officer. The Russians grinned when the British asked what would happen to the officers. Some even drew their fingers across their own throats.

The Cossacks and civilian refugees back at Lienz were given two-days' notice that they were being sent to the Soviet Union and many responded by going on hunger strike. Despite an increased number of British guards at the camp, there were more escapes. There were also more petitions and some Cossacks even dared the British to shoot them on the spot rather than leave the job to the Soviets.

The Cossacks could not believe that their Scottish friends

would betray them. But for the hardened veterans of the Argylls, orders were orders; the Japanese still had to be defeated and they were still soldiers. They knew things would be unpleasant; they did not realise how unpleasant. On 1 June, while other British units moved in to clear the smaller satellite camps, the Argylls went into action at Lienz.

The Argylls found several thousand Cossacks, including approximately 4,000 women and 2,500 children, holding a church service in the camp. People were packed solid around a raised altar which had more than a dozen Orthodox priests on it. A cordon of young Cossack men stood around the crowd.

They believed the British would never break up a church service, but when the Cossacks refused to disperse and get on the trucks that were waiting for them, the Argylls fixed bayonets. Attempts to pull individuals from the crowd failed as the Cossacks linked arms to lock themselves in a single heaving mass of humanity. For the Argylls, fighting the Germans was one thing, but brutalising an unarmed crowd was another.

Eventually, the Argylls managed to cut off a group of around 200 people. So far, no real violence had been used, but now the Cossacks became hysterical and began climbing over each other to escape the clutching hands of the Scottish soldiers. As people started to fall under the feet of the crowd and a human pyramid started to build, the Argylls waded in with pickaxe handles in a bid to pull people to safety and regain control of the situation. As many as six people suffocated at the base of the human pyramid before it could be broken up.

As tempers flared and frustration mounted, the Argylls became freer in their use of the axe handles and the butts of their rifles. Some of the soldiers hit on the tactic of grabbing children and throwing them on the trucks. Then, when their parents broke from the crowd to rescue them, they were grabbed and forced onto the trucks as well. The desperate soldiers were soon knocking people unconscious as they battled to pull people from the seething crowd of panicking Cossacks.

As the seesaw struggle continued, a fence gave way under the weight of humanity pressing against it and many Cossacks made a run for freedom. Some got as far as a nearby wood where they killed themselves rather than face recapture. One mother threw her children off a bridge into the raging waters below and then jumped over the parapet after them. Other Cossacks dived into the River Drau and drowned despite all efforts to save them. The struggle reduced the seasoned soldiers to tears and kneeling Cossacks grabbed their legs and begged to be shot there and then.

A fleet of trucks carried 1,152 people to a waiting rail train where they were locked into boxcars. As the loading continued, the soldiers could hear weeping and moaning from the already filled boxcars. After four hours, a halt was called to that day's repatriations. It has been claimed that as many as 700 people died during the operation. That night more Cossacks and their families escaped from the camp but British efforts to recapture them were half-hearted at best.

The Argylls were braced for more trouble when the loading resumed next day, but the Cossacks had had enough. There was no more resistance. For two days the Argylls shuttled the Cossacks to the Russian Sector. The Soviets announced that they wanted the British trucks as well and there were some tense moments before their drivers were allowed to head back to the Cossack camp again. They could hear the chatter of machine-guns behind them as they headed away from the Russian Sector.

Other British units were involved in forced repatriations from other camps in the area and the actions of some were far more brutal than the Argylls, but most of them had been unfamiliar with the Cossacks and it was the Scots who were remembered as the great betrayers, because they had been regarded as friends.

No-one knows how many people were executed as soon as they were handed over to the Soviets. It is believed that most of the 30,000 or so people deported from the British Sector were sent to slave labour camps in Arctic Russia and Siberia. Only half of them survived the experience and most of them were broken and in poor health as a result of their treatment. The British also turned over 1,000 Germans who had served with the Cossacks to the Soviets. The high-ranking Germans were executed and the rest were enslaved.

The Argylls were cursed by the ragged men, women and children they had helped deport and who were now rotting in the slave camps. The Scots soldiers deserved better from their military and political masters. Fifty years later some spoke to the *Campbeltown Courier* about events in Austria. They wanted their story told, but the British establishment did not. An article written about the repatriation was suppressed by the group editor at the *Oban Times*, a former British Government press officer.

MALAYAN MASSACRE

BATANG KALI 1948

Soldiers kill people. Sometimes they kill the wrong people and sometimes they kill innocent people. The truth about the massacre of around two dozen ethnic Chinese rubber plantation workers in Malaya by the Scots Guards in December 1948 has long been shrouded in mystery. The official version is that the workers were shot trying to escape while being questioned by members of a 14-man Scots Guards patrol looking for Communist insurgents, but why were none of the workers only wounded? Almost before the gunfire stopped echoing around the forest clearing at Batang Kali, questions were being asked. Those questions have never been satisfactorily answered.

Malaya was still a British colony at the time and the authorities there launched an immediate inquiry into the incident. The results were never made public and the only admission a journalist from the English-language newspaper, *The Straits Times,* could get from one senior British official was that 'a bona fide mistake' had been made.

In the early 1970s a second investigation was ordered after some members of the patrol told the *People* newspaper that the plantation workers had indeed been murdered. Scotland Yard was called in by the Labour Government of the time but the investigation was shelved when the Conservatives won a general election not long afterwards.

One has to wonder if the halting of the British police inquiry had anything to do with a desire to hide the truth, because it was the Scots Guards who were involved. The Brigade of Guards is one of the most Conservative (with a capital 'C') units in the British Army. Its officers are drawn from some of the best-connected young men in Britain. When questions were asked again in 2003 about the massacre, a number of former officers sprang to the defence of the Scots Guards. Nearly all were senior members of the Conservative Party or army generals. Strangely, or perhaps not so strangely, the Scotland Yard files on the massacre have vanished.

Perhaps some people feel there is now no point in dredging up events from 1948. However, this ignores the continuing anger felt in Malaya over the massacre and the British cover-up. All recent attempts by the Malaysians to persuade the British Government to come clean about what happened at Batang Kali have been stonewalled. Malayan politicians have compared the massacre to atrocities committed by United States troops in Vietnam and note that at least the American authorities put some of the their men on trial for murdering civilians. The massacre offered an immediate and easy propaganda coup for the Malayan Communist Party and they exploited it to the full. The party was dominated by members of Malaya's minority ethnic Chinese population, which also provided the majority of recruits for the insurgent Malayan Races Liberation Army.

The British had actually trained and supplied the MRLA with weapons during the Second World War when it fought against the Japanese occupation. There had even been promises of independence once Japan was defeated. After the war, the leader of what was then known as the Malayan People's Anti-Japanese Army, Chen Ping, was awarded an OBE for his services to the British Crown. After the Second World War ended, Chen's men buried their British-supplied weapons and waited ... and waited ... and waited.

It was soon clear that the British were dragging their heels on the promise of independence. The Second World War had brought

Britain to the brink of bankruptcy and the tin and rubber produced in Malaya were crucial to the British balance of payments. The British also had problems reconciling the demands of the Malaya community leaders for a curb on the political rights of non-Malayans, especially the Chinese, in the proposed independent state.

Chen's guerrillas started attacking the tin mines and rubber plantations; mine and plantation workers were killed and their British bosses were also targeted. British troops, including the Scots Guards, were brought from Britain and Hong Kong to help protect the mines and plantations. The work involved going into the jungle to find the guerrilla camps. It was dangerous work because the guerrillas, dubbed by the British as Communist Terrorists or CTs, set traps on the jungle trails leading to their camps. One unlucky step by a British soldier could result in instant beheading or a slow painful death impaled on bamboo spikes.

Life at base was not much happier for the mainly conscript British soldiers. The bulk of the Malayan population, particularly the Chinese, was not friendly and neither were the snobbish British settlers – at least not to the rank and file soldiers. Many British troops felt that if they were expected to die protecting the settlers and their economic interests, then the settlers might at least stop treating them as an inferior species. The British community in the colony made it clear the soldiers were only slightly higher up the social ladder than the 'coolies' who worked the rubber plantations. Ordinary soldiers were banned from the settlers' clubs and made unwelcome in many bars and restaurants frequented by them.

The Scots Guards arrived from Hong Kong to be thrown into a brutal and frustrating form of warfare for which they earned few thanks for fighting. They were also poorly trained for the job they were being asked to do. On 11 December, a 14-man patrol from G Company under the command of a sergeant was sent to check out reports of guerrilla activity in the Batang Kali area, north of Kuala Lumpur. Early in the patrol they spotted two men in jungle-green uniforms, who they took for CTs, on a hill about 300 yards ahead of them. The soldiers opened fire, but the two men slipped away into the jungle.

The Scots soldiers were led by their Malayan police guide to a clearing nearby, where a group of ethnic Chinese plantation workers lived in dormitories. The settlement also included a cook house and a building used to store rubber. The soldiers quickly decided they were dealing with Communist sympathisers. Just what led the soldiers to conclude the workers were helping the Communists is unclear. The soldiers later claimed they found ammunition hidden at the settlement. A woman who lived there at the time told a BBC reporter years later that a receipt for fruit was found and the soldiers believed it had been issued by the guerrillas. The 25 men living at the camp were herded into a shed. At this point, the curtain of deceit and cover-up begins to fall over proceedings. The official version is that on the morning of 12 December, the male workers were shot while trying to escape. Why were there no wounded? That was the acid test used by the British when dealing with similar claims from the Nazis during the Second World War.

Another version was soon doing the rounds amongst the British settlers. During the night before the massacre the Scottish soldiers had threatened to start executing their prisoners unless they began providing information about Communist activity in the area. Three of the men were taken out of the shed and shots were heard. In fact the men were moved to another building and shots were fired into the air to trick the other prisoners into believing the executions had begun. The belief that three men had already been executed was said to explain why the plantation workers tried to run off when they were taken from the hut next morning. This story does not explain how the three men supposedly already executed also wound up being shot during the alleged mass escape attempt. A woman who lived in one of the workers' barracks said the Scots did execute one prisoner the night after they arrived. It was the man who had the receipt for the fruit. She said the others were taken from the shed next morning in groups of four or five and shot in cold blood.

There is not even any agreement about how many men were killed. The Malayan policeman who acted as the patrol's guide said he counted 25 bodies, but one man may have survived. Years later, a man called Chong Hong, also identified as Chong Foong, told the Malayan authorities that he was taken out of the shed and told to face away from the British soldiers. But just as they opened fire, he fainted. It is not impossible. The Second World War offers several examples of people surviving machine-gun Nazi death squads because they fainted.

The women were loaded onto trucks and taken away. This raises further questions. Would the British have executed the men in front of the women and then removed them from the scene after they had witnessed the slaughter? Where did the trucks come from and how many more British soldiers were with them? And what of the claims from the women that when they returned to Batang Kali that the mens' bodies had been mutilated?

That a massacre took place is now generally accepted, but who was involved, who ordered it and how far up the chain of command did the responsibility go? Destroying villages believed to be linked to insurgents had long been standard procedure for the British. The use of aeroplanes to bomb villages on the North-West Frontier of India and in the Middle East in the 1920s and 1930s had done away with the need to send out columns of troops to do the job.

In a souvenir booklet prepared for members of the 2nd Battalion who took part in the Malayan campaign, the Scots Guards noted the deaths at Batang Kali in a few short lines.

'Whether it was right or wrong need not concern us at the moment,' it stated. 'Suffice to say that those killed were known to be active bandit sympathisers.'

The booklet notes with evident satisfaction that there was no further trouble in the Batang Kali area for a year after the killings.

A major factor in the eventual defeat of the Malayan Communist insurgency by 1960 was the destruction of villages in the jungle and the transportation of their populations into 'protected settlements'. The settlements were in reality prison camps and many British conscript national servicemen returned home with heartbreaking tales of burning villages to force people into the camps.

Whoever ordered the massacre at Batang Kali was perhaps fortunate that the troops involved were from the politically well-connected Scots Guards. Men from other units involved in less blatant atrocities have been charged and jailed. One regiment's pride, or perhaps something more sinister, is still costing Britain's reputation in the Far East dear.

A HILL IN KOREA

NANTONG RIVER 1950

The Second World War added a new danger to the battlefield – the American air force. US pilots proved almost as great a threat to Allied troops as they were to the Germans. Hundreds of British, American and Canadian troops were killed in attacks by US aircraft after the D-Day landings in 1944 and since 1949 US military pilots have killed around a dozen Scots.

The worst incident came in September 1950 during the Korean War. The Argyll and Sutherland Highlanders were attached to the US 8th Army which was attacking North Korean positions north of the Nantong River. The Argylls had been rushed from their base in Hong Kong to help defeat a Communist invasion of South Korea. The offensive was the Argylls' first real fight of the war. The Argylls' objective was Hill 282. The Scots crept up the scrub-covered hill in the early morning and surprised the North Koreans at breakfast. The fight was brisk and the Argylls were quickly in possession of the hilltop. The Communist's reacted quickly to the loss of the hill and began pounding it with artillery and mortar fire from their positions nearby. The Highlanders found the ground on the hill was hard as concrete and had trouble digging any defensive trenches. Communist North Korean troops were soon swarming down from Hill 388, about a mile away, in a bid to drive the Scots off the hill.

American tanks were supposed to provide support for the Scots but they were badly positioned and proved unable to train their guns on the hoards of enemy heading for Hill 282. The Americans had also promised the Scots artillery support but withdrew it at the last moment to help cover a US attack elsewhere. As the fire from Hill 388 intensified and the Argylls' ammunition began to run low, despite stripping the dead and badly wounded of their bullets, it was decided to call in a US air strike. The call was relayed by a US tactical air controller seven miles away who misidentified Hill 282 as the target. Unaware of this, the Argylls laid out coloured fabric panels to show where their own positions were. The North Koreans also laid out fabric panels. They were the wrong colour but they were enough to confuse the American pilots who responded to the call for an air strike.

A small US scout plane was sent ahead of the main group of US aircraft and reported it was being fired on from Hill 282. It directed the three Mustang fighter-bombers that followed it minutes later to attack the hill. The Mustangs circled the hill and then dived down on it with their machine-guns blazing. Then the American planes pulled out of their dives and released napalm bombs filled with gelled petrol. When these struck the hilltop blossomed with rolling orange flame.

The Argylls who survived being burnt alive started running back to some trenches 50 feet down the slope of the hill. The North Koreans had realised what the Americans were going to do as soon as they saw the Mustangs circling the wrong hill and were already running down Hill 388 to recapture their old positions before the Americans dropped their bombs. Major Kenneth Muir of the Argylls rallied the men who had retreated from the crest and led them back up the hill, along with some reinforcements who had just arrived. Muir and his 30 men were in a race for the blackened summit. A few wounded men on the crest opened fire on the advancing Communists and managed to slow them down enough for Muir and his men to win the race. They found some of the survivors in agonising pain from horrendous burns to as much as 80% of their bodies. Muir found himself holding the North Koreans off with 14 men. The major grabbed a two-inch mortar and began firing it into the advancing Communists. He kept going until he was fatally wounded by two bursts of machine-gun fire. His last words were 'The gooks will never drive the Argylls off this hill'. The Argylls, now numbering only 11 men still capable of firing their weapons, fought on until their ammunition was almost exhausted. When the Bren light machine-guns finally ran out of bullets around 3pm the Argylls pulled back from the crest. The fight for Hill 282 cost the Argylls 17 dead or missing and 76 wounded. An official US account of the fight calculated that two-thirds of the Scots casualties were caused by the Mustangs. The Argylls lost a total of 31 men in Korea.

Muir, the 38-year-old son of a former commanding officer of the Argylls, was awarded a Victoria Cross and an American Silver Star after his death. The British high command wrote the Argylls' casualties off as 'regrettable'. American commanders were relieved that it was not their men who died because they knew if it had been they would have lost their jobs in the wake of public outrage in the USA.

The Americans made the same blunders when the British served alongside them in the First Gulf War in 1991. Three members of the Queen's Own Highlanders were killed when US Air National Guard pilots attacked a convoy of British armoured fighting vehicles in the closing hours of the ground war to liberate Kuwait. Once again the American pilots, who were reservists flying A-10 Warthog 'tankbuster' jets, ignored the fabric panels laid out on the ground to identify the British as allies. The Royal Regiment of Fusiliers lost six men in the same attack.

With wartime friends like these, who needs enemies?

BIBLIOGRAPHY

Anon 1951, *Malaya 1948-51: 2nd Battalion Scots Guards,* published
    privately

Ashley M, 1998, *British Kings and Queens,* Robinson

Ashley M, 1962, *The Greatness of Oliver Cromwell,* Collier

Banham T, 2003, *Not the Slightest Chance: The Defence of Hong
    Kong 1941,* UBC Press

Barber N, 1971, *The War of the Running Dogs,* Collins

Baring Pemberton W, 1964, *Battles of the Boer War,* Batsford

Barnes RM, 1956, *The Uniforms and History of the Scottish
    Regiments,* Seeley Service

Barnes RM, 1950, *A History of the Regiments and Uniforms of the
    British Army,* Seeley

Barnett C, 1971, *Britain and Her Army,* William Morrow &
    Company

Barrow GWS, 1972, *Robert Bruce,* Edinburgh University Press

Baynes J, 1988, *Soldiers of Scotland,* Brassey's

Belchem A, Price R & Evans R (ed) 1996, *The Penguin History of
    Nineteenth Century History,* Penguin

Belfield E, 1975, *The Boer War,* Archon

Bethell N, 1974, *The Last Secret,* Basic Books

Bicheno H, 2003, *Rebels and Redcoats,* Harper Collins

Bowling AH, 1970, *Scottish Regiments and Uniforms,* Almark

Breeze D & Dobson B, 2000, *Hadrian's Wall,* Penguin

Buchan J, 1925, *History of the Royal Scots Fusiliers,* Nelson & Sons

Burgoyne RH, 1883, *Historical Records of the 93rd Highlanders,*
    R Bentley & Son

Callwell CE, 1919, *The Dardenelles,* Houghton Mifflin

Cannon R, 1852, *Historical Record of 71st Foot,*
    Parker Furnival & Parker

Cannon R, 1845, *Historical Record of 42nd Foot ,*
    Parker Furnival & Parker

Cannon R, 1848, *Historical Record of 72nd Foot,*
    Parker Furnival & Parker

Cannon R, 1850, *Historical Record of 74th Foot,*
    Parker Furnival & Parker

Cannon R, 1849, *Historical Record of 21st Foot,*
    Parker Furnival & Parker

Carew T, 1976, *Fall of Hong Kong,* White Lion

Carlyle T, 1904, *The Letters and Speeches of Oliver Cromwell,*
    Methuen

Carruthers B, 2000, *The English Civil Wars,* Cassell & Co,

Carver M, 1999, *The National Army Museum Book of the Boer War,*
    Pan

Carver M, 2003, *The National Army Museum Book of the Turkish
    Front 1914-18,* Pan

Cavendish AEJ, 1928, *The 93rd Highlanders,* privately published

Chandler D, (ed) 1994, *Oxford History of the British Army,*
    Oxford University Press

Chatterton-Newman R, 1992, *Edward Bruce A Medieval Tragedy,*
    Ian Faulkener

Christopher A & Mitrokhin V, 1999, *The Mitrokhin Archive,*
    Penguin

Conan Doyle A, 1901, *The Great Boer War,* Smith

Coogan TP, 2003, *Ireland in the Twentieth Century,* Hutchinson

Curtis E, 1976, *History of Ireland,* Methuen

David S, 1994, *Churchill's Sacrifice of the Highland Division,*
    Brassey's

Davies B, 2001, *The Complete Encyclopedia of the SAS,* Virgin

Deighton L, 1995, *Blood, Tears and Folly*, Pimlico

Duffy C, 1987, *Military Experience in the Age of Reason*, Routledge & Kegan Paul

Duffy C, 2003, *The '45*, Cassell

Fair C, 1971, *From the Jaws of Victory*, Simon & Schuster

Falls C, 1964, *Great Military Battles*, Weidenfield & Nicholson

Farwell B, 1985, *Queen Victoria's Little Wars*, Norton

Featherstone D, 1973, *Colonial Small Wars*, David & Charles

Featherstone D, 1971, *MacDonald of the 42nd*, Seeley Service & Co.

Forbes-Mitchell 1904, *Reminiscences of the Great Mutiny*, MacMillan

Ford J, 1985, *The Brave White Flag*, Richard Drew

Fortescue J, 1899-1930, *History of the British Army (20 Volumes)*, MacMillan & Co.

Fraser D, 1993, *Knight's Cross: A Life of Field Marshal Erwin Rommel*, Harper Collins

Fraser D, 1999, *And We Shall Shock Them*, Cassell & Co.

Glover M, 1973, *Wellington as a Military Commander*, Sphere

Grant R, 1977, *The 51st Highland Division at War*, Ian Allan

Graves D, (ed) 2000, *Fighting for Canada*, Robin Brass Studios

Green H, 1973, *Battlefields of Britain and Ireland*, Constable

Greenhill Gardyne C, 1901, *Life of a Regiment: The Gordon Highlanders*, D Douglas

Hamilton I, 1930, *Gallipoli Diary*, Arnold

Hamilton I, 1944, *Listening for the Drums*, Faber & Faber

Harclode P, 2001, *Fighting Dirty*, Cassell & Co.

Harper JR, 1979, *The Fraser Highlanders*, Montreal Military & Maritime Museum

Hastings M, 1988, *The Korean War*, Pan

Henderson D, 1996, *The Scottish Regiments*, Harper Collins

Hewitson J, 1995, *Scotching the Myths*, Mainstream

Hibbert C, 1978, *The Great Mutiny*, Allen Lane

Higgins RT, 1873, *Records of the King's Own Borderers*, London & Chapman

Holmes R, 2002, *Redcoat,* Harper Collins

Houston RA & Knox WWJ, (ed) 2002, *The New Penguin History of Scotland,* Penguin

Howard P, 1968, *The Black Watch,* Leo Cooper

Howarth D, 1968, *A Near Run Thing,* Collins

James L, 1998, *Raj,* Abacus

James L, 2001, *Warrior Race,* Abacus

Judd D & Surridge K, 2003, *The Boer War,* Palgrave MacMillan

Kaye JW & Malleson GB, 1889, *Kaye's and Malleson's History of the Indian Mutiny,* WH Allan

Keegan J, 2000, *The First World War,* Vintage

Kenyon JP, 1988, *Civil Wars of England,* Knopf

Kirk R, 2004, *Through So Many Dangers,* Robin Brass

Knightly C, 1975, *Flodden,* Almark

Kruger R, 1996, *Goodbye Dolly Gray,* Pimlico

Ladd J, 1992, *Commandos and Rangers of World War II,* Borgo Press

Laffin J 1980, *Damn the Dardenelles,* Osprey

Lehman J, 1972, *The First Boer War,* Jonathan Cape

Linklater E 1942, *The Highland Division,* HMSO

Linklater E & A, 1977, *The Black Watch,* Barrie & Jenkins

MacDonald L, 1997, *1915 Death of Innocence,* Penguin

MacFarlane C, 1853, *History of British India,* G Routledge & Co

Malleson GB, 1892, *The Indian Mutiny of 1857,* Seeley & Co.

Mason P, 1974, *A Matter of Honour,* Jonathan Cape

May R, 1974, *Wolfe's Army,* Osprey

McNair Scott R, 1982, *Robert The Bruce,* Canongate

Mill J, 1990, *The History of British India,* Atlantic

Mitchell C, 1970, *Having Been a Soldier,* Mayflower

Morris J, 1979, *Farewell the Trumpets,* Penguin

Morton G, 2004, *William Wallace Man and Myth,* Sutton

Muir A, 1961, *The First of Foot,* Royal Scots Historical Committee

Neillands R, 1999, *The Great War Generals on the Western Front,* Robinson

Nevinson H, 1919, *The Dardenelles Campaign,* A Holt

Otway AJ, 1980, *History of Medieval Ireland,* E Benn

Pakenham T, 1993, *The Boer War,* Weidenfield & Nicholson

Playfair JSO, 1954, *History of the Second World War in the Middle East,* HMSO

Prebble J, 1967, *Culloden,* Penguin

Prebble J, 1971, *The Lion in the North,* Secker & Warburg

Prebble J, 1977, *Mutiny,* Penguin

Regan G, 1991, *The Guinness Book of Military Blunders,* Guinness

Regan G, 1993, *SNAFU Great American Military Disasters,* Avon

Rhodes James R, 1999, *Gallipoli,* Pimlico

Rose A, 2002, *Kings in the North,* Weidenfield & Nicholson

Ross G, 1995, *Scotland's Forgotten Valour,* MacLean Press

Royal Commission, 1914, *Royal Commission on Landing of Guns at Howth,* HMSO

Royle T, 1982, *Death Before Dishonour,* Mainstream

Royle T, 2004, *The British Civil War,* Little Brown

Schama S, 2000, *A History of Britain,* BBC Worldwide

Seward D, 1978, *The Hundred Years War,* Constable

Seymour W, 1975, *Battles in Britain 1066-1746,* Sidgwick & Jackson

St George Saunders H, 1971, *Green Beret,* New English Library

Steel N & Hart P. 2002, *Defeat at Gallipoli,* Pan

Steel T, 1984, *Scotland's Story,* William Collins

Stewart D, 1977, *Sketches of the Highlanders of Scotland and their Regiments,* John Donald

Story H, 1948, *History of the Cameronians (Scottish Rifles) Vol. II,* Gale & Polden

Sym J, 1962, *Seaforth Highlanders,* Gale & Polden

Tacitus, 1970, *The Agricola,* Penguin

Taylor IC, 1965, *Culloden,* National Trust for Scotland

Thornton E, 1841-45, *A History of the British Empire in India,* WH Allan

Tolstoy N, 1977, *Victims of Yalta,* Hodder & Stoughton

Tomasson K & Buist F, 1967, *Battles of the '45,* Pan

Warner P, 1976, *Famous Scottish Battles,* Fontana

Wood S, 1987, *The Scottish Soldier,* Archive Publications
Woolcombe R, 1980, *All the Blue Bonnets,* Arms & Armour Press
Wrong G, 1918, *The Conquest of New France,* Yale University Press
Young D, 1978, *Rommel The Desert Fox,* Harper & Row
Young P, 1969, *Commando,* Ballantine